HAND-PAINTING
CHINA

HAND-PAINTING CHINA

HOW TO DESIGN AND PAINT YOUR OWN BEAUTIFUL
CERAMICS, WITHOUT THE NEED FOR KILN-FIRING

LESLEY HARLE
AND SUSAN CONDER
PHOTOGRAPHS BY DEBBIE PATTERSON

LORENZ BOOKS

NEW YORK • LONDON • SYDNEY • BATH

**To my mother and father,
Anne and Richard Harle**

First paperback edition published
in 1995 by Lorenz Books
an imprint of Anness Publishing Limited
1 Boundary Row
London SE1 8HP

ISBN 1-85967-136-5

Publisher: **Joanna Lorenz**
Designer: **Lisa Tai**
Styled Photography: **Debbie Patterson**
Step-by-Step Photography: **Zul Mukhida**

Printed and bound in Hong Kong

NOTE ON PAINTING CERAMICS

This book contains all the information on the paints, techniques and materials you need to create beautiful pieces of decorated china. The projects are designed to be painted with special ceramic paints and glazes that can be fixed, or 'fired', in a domestic oven. However, it is important that you take care over the selection and application of these paints. Firstly, as there is a wide range of products on the market, and they are constantly being refined and developed, be sure to study the manufacturer's instructions about the use of the paint product in question.

Secondly, all the paints recommended in this book are suitable for painting decorative objects. Ensure, however, that the painted or varnished surfaces of such items will not come into contact with the mouth, food or drink. The paints and glazes are not food-safe, and so due care should be taken. If you do want to use an item for food, design it so that 'contact' areas are left unpainted, or adapt the project so that it is suitable for kiln-firing (see page 156). Various ways of adapting projects are suggested through the text.

CONTENTS

INTRODUCTION

This book is all about designing and creating your own hand-painted ceramics, and using them to match or complete interior design effects. In the past, the facility to paint ceramics was limited to professional designers with access to a kiln, but now exciting ranges of paints are available which can be 'set' or fixed in an ordinary oven. For the first time, everyone has everything they need to create beautiful decorated china in their own home. The results are durable and washable, so the items are perfect for practical use as well as presentation and display.

The advantage of designing and painting your own china is not only the thrill of creating something beautiful and unique, but the possibilities it opens up in interior design. Both an inspirational guide and a practical manual, this book is full of imaginative ideas on how to use ceramics as an element of personal style. When painting your own china, you are no longer restricted to the endless searching through shops and markets for the 'perfect' accessory to match a decor, but can create a piece of art that exactly meets your requirements.

Imaginative suggestions are given in the following pages for using ceramics in many ways. As well as unusual items of crockery, plates and bowls, there are individually painted tiles for the kitchen and bathroom, picture and mirror frames, tiles used on sills, trunks and tables, window boxes, flower vases, storage and apothecary jars, boxes, jugs, and much more. Practical step-by-step projects are given, fully photographed, and of course ideas and techniques can be taken from one suggestion and applied to another.

On a practical level, hand-painting china requires no specialized large-scale equipment, and there are sections in the book on all the basic ceramic painting techniques, equipment and materials that you will need. Information is also given on how to maintain and care for the finished objects: the creative pleasure of painting ceramics doesn't stop when you put your paints away – you can enjoy living with your own hand-decorated china for many years, and may even create a few new family 'heirlooms'.

Innovative, accessible and the first of its kind, *Designer China* will open the doors of a new craft that can be directly integrated into your home and personal style.

A plain wooden trunk or chest is transformed by a layer of hand-painted tiles (opposite). The repeated design is inspired by Portuguese and Spanish-style motifs, as are the classic colours of Mediterranean blue and white. To paint and mount tiles, see the project on page 128.

DESIGN AND INSPIRATION

Sources of inspiration for decorating ceramics are limitless, and although naturally creative people can often find inspiration from within their own imagination, there are also many objects in the everyday world that can be used as the springing point for design. If anything, there is a surfeit, rather than a lack.

Inspiration can be as vague as the colours of ceramic paints as they sit on the palette, or as a piece of music, or as precise as the patterns of an old Aran-knit or the colours of a contemporary 'designer' sweater. You can always, of course, try to repeat exactly the existing design of one object onto another, but as you become more experienced and confident in painting ceramics, you'll find that you are seeking inspiration from, rather than copying, a design, and perhaps drawing on several sources of inspiration simultaneously, instead of just one.

Collecting prints and postcards of works of art, such as these postcards of Matisse paper cut-outs (right), can be creative springboards for colour, form and subject matter. See, for instance, the Matisse-inspired platter (above, and with a vase on page 18).

SOURCES OF INSPIRATION

Design ideas can come from the object to be decorated: a fish- or star-shaped serving plate is an obvious example. Inspiration can come from the purpose of the object to be decorated; a dinner service or tea set to be displayed over the Christmas holiday, for example, instantly calls to mind a wealth of Christmas symbolism.

If you know or have decided on the room in which the china is to be displayed or used, you can exactly co-ordinate the colours to a specific decor. A rich red and gold decor in a dining room might suggest an elaborately decorative red and gold Indian paisley pattern, or, more simply, red and gold Regency stripes. A bathroom can be decorated with tiles painted with a marine or nautical theme — alternating scallop shells, starfish, cowrie shells or the paraphernalia of boats, for example; a conservatory can be decorated with tiles bearing a flower or leaf motif.

Colour and pattern ideas can come from a particular period in history, such as the mid-nineteenth century Arts and Crafts Movement, with its simple, fresh designs based on natural forms, and its emphasis on quality craftsmanship. Associated in England with William Morris, in America Candace Wheeler, Margaret Whiting and Ellen Miller were the main proponents of the similar Craftsman, or Mission, Style. You might have a favourite historical period which you want to evoke in newly painted 'instant antique' china; the highly popular Art Nouveau, with its slender tendrils and arabesques, is one such option, or Art Deco, with its angular, squat, heavy forms. You may have a room decorated predominantly in one particular period style, and want a china design that blends in or reflects elements of that era. There are many museums that specialize in or are strong in domestic design, which provide excellent sources of reference and inspiration – such as the Victoria and Albert Museum in London; the American Museum in Britain, Bath, England; the Museum of American Folk Art in New York; the Philadelphia Museum of Art; the Metropolitan Museum of Art in New York City; the Shelburne Museum, in Shelburne, Vermont; and The Henry Ford Museum, in Dearborn, Michigan. Contemporary potteries and craft

Shells are as varied in colour and form as flowers, and ideal subjects for decorating ceramics with aquatic connotations, such as the bathroom tiles illustrated on page 84. Scallop shells are good to start with, since their flat, simple shapes are easy to copy.

A good-quality gift, stationery or museum shop is a goldmine of inexpensive inspiration. Wrapping paper, covered boxes, cards, posters and prints can provide subjects, colourways and stylistic direction.

Poppies, rich paisley fabrics and tea leaves inspired the subtle colours and pattern of this decorative tea set. The white rims, handles and spouts add a sparkling note of contrast (to make, see project on page 114).

shops, ethnic craft shops and even the china sections in big department stores are all worth visiting.

One type of ceramic decoration can inspire another. Old-fashioned Italian apothecary jars, for example, hand-painted with floral designs in combinations of orange, yellow, blue, green and white, could inspire the colour scheme and motif for newly decorated tiles. Displaying them, or ones you paint yourself, against the tiles, is an obvious finishing touch.

Inspiration can be geographic or cultural in origin, whether local or exotic. The hot countries of annual vacations and holidays, where the bright, fierce sunlight complements the higher-key colour schemes, could be one source. Although a high degree of detail is possible with ceramic painting, for most people a plain, direct style is easiest to master, and many Mediterranean, African and South American cultures can provide visually strong but simple designs.

Two-dimensional sources

Any two-dimensional design is a potential source of inspiration and direct reference. Paper patterns in particular can provide dramatic colour and design starting points. Out-of-date wallpaper sample books are well worth having, just for flicking through from time to time. Intricate designs on white backgrounds can be simplified for copying by painting out some details or parts of motifs with masking-out fluid. A pair of white cardboard L-shapes or 'right-angles' can be used together to frame a particular area of detailed wallpaper, so you can 'crop' an intricate or over-elaborate pattern into a more manageable one.

Old papers and wrapping papers are valuable as sources of pattern, especially if you want to paint china to match a specific period or style. Some museums have collections of old wallpapers on display, and some manufacturers do accurate reproductions of period wallpapers. And in the last few years, gift wrapping paper has been successfully marketed in tear-out, portfolio form, each portfolio based on a specific theme, such as American quilts, turn-of-the-century Vienna style (Wienerwerkstätte), Japanese kimono fabrics, Art Nouveau, English floral chintzes, traditional paisley and Art Deco, and on the work of artists, such as Raoul Dufy, with a particularly decorative graphic style. Design sourcebooks are also available, illustrating the designs of particular decorative artists; Owen Jones' *Grammar of Ornament* is one of the classic visual references for pattern ideas.

Likewise, decorative fabrics can provide fertile hunting ground. Most fabric shops and sections of department stores have remnants bins or tables, where small pieces of fabric are sold off cheaply. Ferreting through jumble or rummage sales for fabric scraps can often be rewarding, for both colour schemes and patterns. Even a small section of Oriental carpet, carefully observed, can become the inspiration for colour schemes or shapes, as can American-style patchwork quilts, crewel embroidery, rag rugs, North and South American Indian weaving, the dhurries and other crafts of the Indian sub-continent.

Changes in techniques or media,

Provençal fabrics, with their bright colours and simple floral and geometric motifs, are ideal source material for decorating ceramics in the Provençal style. A border pattern and widely-scattered, tiny motifs on a flat, solid ground are as effective on a jug, bowl or plate as they are on a length of fabric. For a project based on the Provençal style, see the spice jars on page 76.

such as basing a design for your hand-painted china on a particular knitting stitch or pattern, automatically affects the finished design, and can lead to unexpectedly rich results. (On the other hand, designs may on occasion 'translate' badly from one medium or technique to another, and you will need to be flexible enough to change or develop the design as necessary.)

Old tiles are well worth studying, and of course you may want to reproduce these original 'designer ceramic' pieces on modern china-ware, for an antique look at a fraction of the cost. Ancient Egyptian tiles, lining the tombs of the Pharaohs and other dignitaries, depict charming, everyday scenes, such as hunting and family gatherings; early Persian tiles covered walls with blue and green patterns of leaves, flowers and birds, equal in richness to Persian carpets; and later, as the influence of Chinese tiling spread West, intricate, complex geometric patterns in blue and white appeared. Isfahan, Iranian and Medieval English tiles, initially used for paving cathedrals, abbeys and royal buildings, were mostly of geometric pattern, often divided up into four, sometimes more, and depicting heraldic devices, fleur-de-lis, rosettes or armorial images. Opaque tin glaze, or majolica, with its bright colours, is seen at its best in the exquisite devotional tiled panels and pavements done by the Renaissance sculptor Luca della Robbia.

Sixteenth-century Dutch blue and white Delftware is world famous for its depiction of everyday life with clean simplicity, humour and realism; Dutch Royal Makkum tiles are notable for their rich colour and detail. Transfer-printed English and American Victorian tiles featured flowers, leaves, birds and animals, as well as myths, geometric designs, Western and Oriental landscapes, and even popular actors and actresses of the day. Museums with permanent displays of tiles include the Victoria and Albert Museum, London; the City Museum, Stoke-on-Trent; the Gladstone Pottery Museum, Longton, Staffordshire; and the Ironbridge Gorge Museum, Telford, Shropshire. In America, Victorian tiles from the Low Art Tile Company, which made 'natural' tiles by impressing a real leaf or stem into the wet clay then glazing the impression, can be found in specialist and local museums, along with tiles from the Rookwood Pottery in Cincinnati, Ohio.

Art, especially the art of the last hundred years or so, is a rich source of inspiration. Henri Matisse's huge paper cut-outs of dancers, for example, show how powerful simple shapes

'Blue and white' cuts across historical and cultural styles, and is as much Chinese or Dutch as Persian, English, Provençal, Portuguese, American or Japanese. The feeling of cool, fresh, clean airiness the colours convey together is always restful and pleasing.

This platter and jug, with their bright colours and fluid, abstract patterns, were inspired by Matisse cut-outs. Sticky templates are cut out of masking paper and stuck randomly on the objects, then the background and motifs are painted in bold blocks of contrasting colour. When the paint is dry, the masking paper is peeled off. You could, if wished, colour-wash second-hand furniture to match.

can be. Bold, intense colour combinations are the keynote of the paintings of the Fauves: Matisse, Gauguin, Cézanne, Rouault, Vlaminck, Braque and Derain. The primary-colour geometry of Piet Mondrian, the mythical pattern-making in lush colours of Paul Klee, the flowing rainbows of colour from the American painter Morris Louis, and the more precise, geometric colour studies of his compatriot artists, Frank Stella and Ellsworth Kelly — all these explore the interaction of colour and form, and are as relevant to the ceramics painter as to the artist or art student.

DESIGN AWARENESS

Try to be open to design influence from all directions, rather than just considering tightly defined periods. Visiting National Trust properties in

England, Scotland and Wales, or historic Williamsburg in America, can be richly rewarding if you store away in your mind some design 'snippets'; perhaps a small group of colours that went well together, or a motif that you particularly liked. Ethnic shops, whether Oriental, Indian, African or South American, are treasure troves of colour and pattern ideas.

With the increasing interest in interior design, contemporary and historical, Eastern and Western, and in so-called primitive cultures as well as highly sophisticated ones, there is a plethora of reasonably priced illustrated books and lifestyle magazines, catalogues, postcards and objects available. Collect what pleases you visually, even if you have no specific use for it; sooner or later it may influence your design. In the field of decorative arts, nothing is too mundane: well-designed food packaging, for example, can be as valid a source of inspiration as a famous painting.

Many man-made sources of inspiration are themselves based on natural forms, and you can always go direct to nature: to plant forms in general, leaves, flowers, berries, fruits, seed heads and pods, mineral rocks, animals, feathers, shells, landscapes, seascapes and even skyscapes. The colour schemes of the natural world are an ongoing sourcebook of ideas. The autumn leaf colours in an English or (even more so) New England countryside, for example, range from the pale yellow of birch to the deep burgundy of some maples and beeches. Fashion designers draw on natural, seasonal colours for their collections and the same rich source is open to ceramic designers.

Geometry is as much a part of nature as abstract form is: consider the unique and intricate beauty of the snowflake or crystal formations under a microscope. If you are keen on a geometric approach, look through a kaleidoscope or optical toy, available from some natural history museums, that reproduces the multi-faceted vision of a fly, for inspiration; even the most mundane room setting becomes fragmented into intriguing, interlocking shapes. Patterns created by a kaleidoscope can be extremely intricate, but you can easily isolate, in your mind's eye, three or four attractive interlinked shapes. Many people find geometrical designs, with their rigid boundary definitions, easier to start with than freehand ones, which depend on a certain amount of confident brushwork to be effective.

COLOUR

Colour is subjective, a way of expressing yourself and demonstrating your personal taste and style. If you feel comfortable or pleased with the finished effect, then it's right for you.

Fruit translates easily from three to two dimensions, as a decorative motif for fabrics, papers and china. Simple, orderly repetition of a single fruit and its leaf, such as the strawberries and foliage on the gold, black and red jug, is one approach; mix-and-match clusters of fruit, such as on the Twenties plate, another.

Colour is so much a part of every-day life that it is easy to ignore its importance or take it for granted. Because you see colour wherever you look, you tend not to 'see' it at all. Working with colour on ceramics, however, is a small-scale activity, enabling you to focus the eye and the mind onto something manageable and totally controllable.

Understanding colour

Using colour is not a matter of hard and fast rules, but understanding the basics, and a few guidelines, can help you create the effect you want. Colour is made by light waves reflecting off objects. These waves contain a spectrum: the yellow, orange, red, violet, blue and green of the rainbow. A coloured surface absorbs some parts of the spectrum and reflects others. A red tablecloth, for example, absorbs all the colours of the spectrum except red, which it reflects. A dominating colour, it should be used with care.

Like flowers, fruit is a rich source of ideas, whether humble garden apples or exotic rarities. Try halving fruit for inspiration for abstract designs; cross sections through pomegranates, for example, are richly intricate, and cross sections through lemons and limes beautiful in their geometry. Try, too, to include the leaves which often, as in the case of strawberries, are as ornamental as the fruit itself. For a project based on fruit and its leaves, see the fruit bowl on page 92.

Hand-painted tiles in single colours have a subtle variation in tone that is not possible on mass-produced ones. By painting your own, you increase the range of colours from which to choose.

The primary colours, magenta (red), blue and yellow, are theoretically the basis of all other colours, although with ceramic paints, having a selection of blues, reds and yellows enlarges your options for mixing colours. The secondary colours, orange, green and violet, are made by mixing two primaries. Secondary colours mixed with primary colours create tertiary colours: yellow-orange, blue-green, and so on. The primary, secondary and tertiary colours are pure hues, since they contain no white or black. Once any of these colours is mixed with white, it becomes a tint; mixed with black, it becomes a shade.

The colour wheel

Joining up the colours of the spectrum, end to end, forms a colour circle or wheel, with each primary colour progressing into the next one, and with a secondary colour in between. Colours that are next to each other on the colour wheel, such as yellow, yellow-green and green, are called 'harmonious', since they can be juxtaposed without clashing. Colours opposite one another on the colour wheel, such as blue and orange, or yellow and violet, are called 'complementary' colours, and contrast well with one another. Contrasting schemes tend to be livelier than harmonious ones. Traditionally, one contrasting or complementary colour should be used only as an accent for the other. If used in equal amounts, two complementary colours can fight and even set up a glare, a technique much used to deliberate effect in Op Art paintings of the Sixties. You may want this effect, or want to avoid it.

Neutral colours, such as grey and beige, are subtle on their own, or can provide a peaceful background for livelier hues. Grey can be made of

Bright orange pumpkins, golden grain and pale earthenware tones capture the spirit of Thanksgiving and harvest festivals. A pretty jug does not need to be painted with a pattern to transform it – here, an all-over coating of deep cream ages it in a country way.

varying proportions of black and white, but a hint of another colour or colours can give grey a warm or cool cast, and a distinct character. Beiges contain white and brown, itself a mixture of many colours. There is a huge range of greys, and neutral colours generally, depending on the exact proportion of white, black and the hues used to make them. As in fashion, neutral colours have an important role to play in ceramic decoration.

The qualities of colour

Yellow, orange and red are traditionally 'warm' colours, creating a feeling of visual heat. Blue, green and violet are 'cool' colours, for the opposite reason. The definitions, however, merge at the boundaries, with acid yellow having a distinctly cool tone, and violets with a high red content appearing warm. Warm colours tend visually to dominate cool ones, coming toward your eye, whereas cool colours recede. Again, there are exceptions: a milky, pale 'cool' blue will dominate a 'warm' crimson.

As well as temperature, colours have tones. These are graded according to their white or black content. Tints with a high white content, such as peach or lemon yellow, are tonally light; naturally deep colours, such as pure blue, or those with black added, are tonally dark. You can get interesting and subtle results by using tonally

A Medieval-style plate based on the fleur-de-lis motif. Easy geometric alternatives include vertical or diagonal crosses, diamonds, zigzags, chevrons or crescents. See page 124 for project instructions.

This boldly-painted vase, with its floral motif reminiscent of Forties-style fabrics, is inspired by sumptuous, fully-open camellia blooms. Loose brushstrokes, overlapping layers of colour and rough leaf and flower shapes, each one slightly different, give the design its relaxed, informal appeal. Remember, painting ceramics is quite different from taking photographs, and capturing the spirit of what you draw is more important than reproducing it accurately.

To execute this design, roughly draw the flowers onto the vase with a soft pencil, in an even pattern. Paint the flowers and then the leaves, adding the darker shades of the colours later, once the main painting has dried. Use rough, random brushstrokes.

similar colours, such as maroon and deep navy blue, together, but you also run the risk of a flat effect.

Colour is not seen in isolation, but is affected by surrounding colours. A hot pink, for example, takes on a bluish tinge when surrounded by red, and takes on a reddish tinge when surrounded by blue. Even the apparent size of an area of colour is affected by its surroundings. A yellow square on a violet background will appear visually larger than an identically sized violet square on a yellow background. Likewise colour and scale: a small amount of bright orange, for example, can be exciting, but a large amount may be overwhelming or aggressive. Pure hues, such as the red, blue and yellow of the spectrum, are bright and fresh but also potentially dominating. On the other hand, they are ideal for miniprints, where the proportion of decoration or motif to the background is small. Tints, such as pink, lavender and pale blue; and shades, such as midnight blue and olive green, tend to be easy to accommodate in multicolour schemes, although schemes composed entirely of tints or shades can be dull without a lively touch of bright colour.

The amount and quality of light affect colour. Plum purple, for example, can look rich or depressing, depending on the amount of light. Colours look different in natural daylight from artificial light, and incandescent, tungsten-halogen and fluorescent lights affect various colours differently. In the larger sense, the soft

grey, misty dull English light is undoubtedly related to the usual English palette of soft, pale colours in landscape, architecture and interior design. In contrast, the intense bright light of hotter countries can be similarly related to their use of bright sunny colours, both for exterior and interior use.

A simple design based on rich Colonial colours; the broad, blue-painted vertical bands vary in width according to the width of the jug, and are positioned to fit within the decorative vertical ridges of the ceramics. These ridges provide a natural edge to paint against, but if you feel more comfortable, use masking tape. The hand-painted, thin black lines add crisp detail, and also align with the ceramic ridges.

Working with colour

You can use colour to create moods. The same pattern can be electrifying, soothing or mournful, according to the choice of colours. A vase decorated in lemon yellow, lime green and cobalt blue, for example, looks modern and bright; the same pattern carried out in dull pink, olive green and yellow ochre looks much softer and more traditional.

If you are new to working with colours, spend a few days experimenting with watercolours, poster paints or gouache and an artist's sketchpad. Just paint dabs of colour against one another, trying unusual juxtapositions as well as traditional combinations or ones you feel 'safe' with. You may be surprised at what works together for you and what doesn't.

Try, too, mixing colours to obtain new ones. As well as being creative, it is also economical, since a palette of basic, key colours plus black and white can provide a huge range of variations. Try a series of six or eight graduated tonal changes, such as alizarin crimson, with more and more white added, until the final sample has just a hint of pink. Try mixing three colours together in various proportions – the number of variations is infinite. You will soon discover that the more colours that are added to a mixture, the muddier it

becomes. This is not to say that all colours must be bright. Earth colours such as raw umber and burnt sienna can be sombre and fresh at the same time, and such colours, highlighted with touches of primary colours, in fact form the basis of many cultures' decorative style.

PATTERN

Decorative pattern is not necessary to human survival, but it has enlivened our surroundings since time immemorial, and the creation of patterns, for those who do it, is as enjoyable as the pleasure gained from the finished design.

The urge to make patterns is as old and instinctive as civilization itself. As well as the soothing physical process of repeating hand movements again and again, there is the pleasure of living with the finished design. In daily life, we surround ourselves with patterned wallpaper, curtains, upholstery, carpets, china, cutlery and clothing. In spite of the easy accessibility of cheap manufactured goods, the pattern-based crafts of hand-knitting, weaving, basket-making and pottery are popular pastimes. In the last few years, the hand-stencilling, marbling, rag-rolling, combing, stippling and sponging of textural patterns onto surfaces have also become increasingly popular and

White china blanks don't have to be plain – search out white ceramic crockery items with attractive raised relief borders and features. As sharp and clean-looking as fresh lemons, this yellow and green bas-relief jug and plate project is perfect for beginners, since the shapes are there to follow with a paintbrush, and any slight mistakes only add to its hand-painted charm (see project on page 72).

Tartan plaids inspired the design of these hand-painted plates, and the rich wool colourways of red and green. There are dozens of plaid designs you could choose from – a tartan swatch book is well worth obtaining.

widespread, and all of which can be translated onto ceramics.

Pattern is decorative design or ornament, usually on a flat surface such as a wall, carpet, fabric or plate. Repetition is the primary characteristic of pattern, with similar forms or groupings recurring at regular intervals; any line or shape repeated often enough forms a pattern. Man-made patterns, as opposed to natural patterns such as pebbles on a beach or daisies on a lawn, tend to occur within given boundaries, whether the width of fabric or wallpaper, or the circumference of a vase. These limitations affect the scale and design of the pattern, since the repeat should ideally occur imperceptibly, with no obvious beginning or ending.

Pattern can be a natural outgrowth of methods of workmanship: the processes of weaving, plaiting and net-making, for example, create pattern which can have an ornamental value beyond its practical one. Pattern can be tribal; patterns in primitive weavings often distinguish the village or even the family of an object's origin. Scotch tartans originally denoted a specific clan; today they are divorced from tribal associations, and are largely decorative. Other patterns are religious in origin; much Islamic calligraphic design, in its many styles

and with intricate beauty, is an elaborate rendering of verses from, or references to, the Koran.

Patterns often hark back to older patterns. The eighteenth-century wallpaper and fabric pattern makers, for example, often drew heavily on the patterns of antique Oriental, Indian, Kashmiri and Turkish shawls and carpets as their starting points. In designing patterns, using other patterns as inspiration is a traditional and accepted approach. You can always modify, substitute or interpret the theme in a different way, and even changing a single colour or a minor detail can create an entirely unique result.

On a practical level, many patterns had their origins in concealing poor-quality materials or fabrics, in the way that textured anaglypta wallpaper conceals poor plasterwork. In painting ceramics, you can use pattern to conceal cracks or mends, and even turn a flaw into a design inspiration. Crazes in the glaze could be formalized by overpainting some or all of them with colour in contrast to the base colour, using a very fine, pointed brush. Chips could be concealed much more effectively with stippling in a contrasting colour than by attempting to match exactly the base colour. A diagonal hairline crack

Spices from the Near and Far East, such as saffron, cinnamon, ginger and turmeric, provide richly authentic colour guides for a paisley-inspired design. Reference for the paisley pattern, based on the traditional curled teardrop shape, is easily available from the numerous fabrics, especially silk scarves, based on nineteenth-century paisley. If you are really keen, there are entire design sourcebooks devoted to paisley patterns, and a collection of paisley patterns in Paisley, Scotland. (See the paisley teapot project on page 114.)

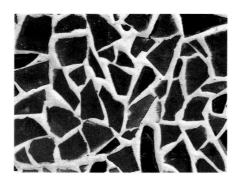

Natural-coloured putty is used here as the 'background' for a mosaic mirror frame. Putty is available in several colours, and you could use blue or black, or a contrasting third colour, instead. (See the complete project on page 110.)

This Greek embroidered cut-work is based on flower and leaf forms, simplified into geometric shapes. The beige and white can be reversed for ceramic painting, with narrow borders and floral motifs in beige on a glazed white ground – a lovely idea for a jug to match a tablecloth or place mats and napkins. You can use this pattern as inspiration for tiles, too, repeating each square of fabric on an individual tile.

could inspire a diagonal design, with a solid colour on one side of the crack and two-toned, stippled, marbled or sponged colour on the other.

Patterns can be bold or delicate, warm or cool, comfortable or awesome, according to the choice of colours, scale and imagery. Patterns can enrich the environment or overwhelm it; although it is appealing to have co-ordinated designs throughout your interior, too much 'perfect matching' can be oppressive, and it might be preferable to take just an element of an overall pattern to develop on your china design.

One of the keys to successful use of pattern in interior design is in fact in providing occasional relief from it, in proportion to its strength. Tiny mini-prints, for example, can be used, mixed and matched in a more relaxed way than large-scale patterns such as the classic William Morris fabric and wallpaper pattern, 'Golden Lily Minor'.

Tile patterns need special thought. What looks perfect as a self-contained pattern on a single tile could be overwhelming when placed next to identically patterned tiles. The delicate corner motifs on many Delft tiles, for example, create a sense of unity seen *en masse*, but if the corner motifs or borders are heavy or crude, they could visually dwarf the central image once the tiles are *in situ*.

Basic types of pattern

Patterns can be representational, interpretive, geometric or abstract. Representational, or realistic, images are intended to capture the three-dimensionality and detailed quality of an object, in the same way that a botanical illustration or photograph does. In ceramics, for example, meticulously depicted roses and other garden flowers, observed directly from nature, were popular transfer-print patterns in Victorian times. Painted representational patterns are the most challenging to do. They are done free-hand and it requires a high degree of technical skill to create a three-dimensional effect on a two-dimensional surface; think, for example, of capturing the depth in the petals of a fully open rose. It also involves mixing paints to get correct shades and tints of various hues, for shadows and highlights. If you are already skilled in painting, then it is easy to transfer from watercolour, oil or acrylic to ceramic paints. Several design ideas based on realistic images are suggested through the book, but no detailed, step-by-step instructions are given, because these designs rely on a higher degree of artistic skill and

experience than can be covered in practical instructions.

Interpretive patterns, as opposed to realistic patterns, are based on natural objects, such as animals or flowers, but are simplified in appearance, almost like paper doll cut-outs or Pennsylvania Dutch appliqués. Interpretive patterns aim to capture the essence of the subject, rather than every minute detail, and are not judged according to how closely they resemble the original, but on their own innate attractiveness. The designs in this book are interpretive,

rather than realistic, since interpretive art is within everyone's ability. Children are particularly good at it, since — while lacking the sophisticated skills needed for representational art — they lack the self-consciousness that often inhibits adults from drawing freely what they see or feel.

In contrast, patterns can be geometric, as in the simple Greek motifs based on crenellations, or the highly intricate and elaborate patterns on tiles in Islamic architecture. Pure mathematical geometry is a

Spongeware is as easy to do as it is enchanting, and blue on white is a traditional combination. By varying the size, shape and texture of the sponges, you can create a whole range of marks, and you can vary the proportion of white to blue according to taste.

main source of pattern, and can be developed to varying degrees of complexity.

Abstract geometric patterns may have been inspired by some natural object, but their original source of inspiration has evolved to such an extent that it is no longer recognizable. Other abstract patterns can be literally derived from thin air: a loosely held pencil making randomly overlapping figures, for example, or the spatters of paint from a flicked, paint-laden brush.

Variations on pattern

There is a fine dividing line between patterns and textures, in which the surfaces of objects are represented artistically: *faux* marble, malachite, tortoiseshell and bamboo, for example. Because these techniques, together with stippling and sponging, create an all-over effect, with similar but not identical weight and detail over a potentially indefinite area, many people find these textures easier to do than patterns requiring mathematical precision or representational accuracy. They can also start, end, and meet almost anywhere.

Akin to patterns are series, groups of individually distinct motifs with a common related subject. The Victorian tile-makers produced hundreds of series to meet popular demand. Minton's 'Rustic Figures' series, for example, included a woman carrying a bucket over a stream, a seated girl with goats, children with a puppy, a shepherd at rest under a tree, a boy in a stream, hay-raking and a little girl

feeding a pet rabbit. There were historical series, series based on the Old and New Testaments, Dutch and English landscapes, Shakespeare characters, fables, fairy tales, nursery rhymes, elves, water nymphs, days of the week, months and seasons of the year, the Seven Ages of Man, signs of the Zodiac, dogs' heads, birds, hunting and fishing scenes, sea shells, scenes of Oriental daily life, natural history, Chaucer, Scott's novels, and so on. Today, many of these subjects would be considered too obscure to use as a decorative theme, but others, such as game birds, cookery ingredients or modern-day children's cartoon characters, make ideal subjects for series. Each decorated item becomes a mini-painting, and though the individual subjects are different, a consistent approach to style and colour should be taken.

PLANNING A DESIGN

When choosing a representational, interpretive, geometric or abstract style, remember that there is no hierarchy; whatever you enjoy painting, looking at and living with is right for you. On the other hand, every now and then it is nice to try a different style, just to avoid getting into a design rut. You may find that spending a week on geometric or abstract patterns enlivens your work when you return to a more realistic approach, or vice versa.

If you see painting ceramics as a form of fine art, then the chosen colours and design should have a self-contained integrity, wherever it is displayed; after all, Picasso, Miró,

The pattern on this jug was taken from the well known paisley motif, and the colours from Indian spices (to paint, see the project on page 114).

Dufy and Chagall – who all painted ceramics in the Twenties – treated blank pots as canvas, and didn't colour co-ordinate them to particular rooms. If, however, you see it as an extension of interior design, then the decor, mood and colour scheme of the room should strongly influence the style. In a sunny, bright yellow room, for example, you could paint the vase yellow, but add small touches of lime green and cobalt blue to add interest.

If you do have a room in mind, choose the ceramic objects or tiles to be decorated with an eye to their ultimate position. Tiles, for example, need specific surfaces devoted to them, while three-dimensional objects, such as vases, look best with space around them (the equivalent of 'working white' in graphic design). They should also be placed so they are safe from accidental knocks.

Have the object in front of you when considering the design, ideally in the room in which it is to go; if not, relevant swatches of fabric, wallpaper and paint cards are helpful, as well as any other references you need, such as an existing picture or pattern.

Stick to simple designs to start with, such as abstract or geometric patterns, or even curving brush-strokes. Within the pattern itself, it is important to consider the gaps, the 'negative' spaces between the 'positive' images, since they can be equally powerful visually. If you are doing a group of objects, such as a tea set, try to keep the proportion of background to pattern roughly the same for each object. Once you feel confident and experienced, you can try more complex or realistic images.

These elegant grey-green and gold verdigris-effect candleholders are painted using the method shown on page 154. The colours are chosen to match the Art Nouveau-inspired tablecloth and glasses. Virtually any colour and gold combine well, but you could substitute silver, copper or bronze metallic paint instead.

CERAMICS THROUGH THE HOME

Opportunities for using and displaying decorated ceramics in the home are as unlimited as your own imagination, and designer effects can be achieved on a shoestring budget.

Designer china can be incorporated into any room in the home, whatever its size, style or purpose. While tiling is usually associated with bathrooms and kitchens, it can be used and decorated creatively in many other locations, such as conservatories, utility rooms and entrance halls; tile or mosaic entrance halls were standard features in Victorian homes, as were tiled fireplace surrounds. Ceramic crockery is naturally at home in the kitchen and dining room, but as decorated *cache pots* holding potted plants, vases holding flowers or purely as *objets d'art*, ceramic artefacts can be displayed almost anywhere. Shallow plates could double as wall plaques; bowls could hold pot-pourri; jugs could hold dried flowers.

The colour scheme of this charming country bedroom (right), with its blue-sponged walls and blue and white linen, is repeated in blue and white spongeware, and provides the perfect contrast for sunny yellow daffodils. The spring colours of the plate (above) would blend well in such a room decor, or work equally well in a bright kitchen.

DESIGNER CHINA ROOM BY ROOM

This chapter is divided, for easy reference, into separate rooms, but many of the ideas given for one room can be adapted for another. Shelving as presentation space, for example, is common to many rooms, as are windowsills — always a potential display place for decorated tiles themselves, and ceramic objects. Then, too, decorative motifs on china can link areas of the home together. With open-plan homes, this is often a good way of increasing the feeling of spatial unity. Dining room and kitchen areas, for example, often flow freely into each other in modern layouts, and carrying a decorative motif through both gives each the appearance of more generous space. The wallpaper motif in a master or children's bedroom can be repeated as a painted motif on the bath tiles or even soap dish in a bathroom; a decorated tile border inset into a dining room floor can be repeated on plant pots in an adjoining conservatory.

KITCHENS AND DINING ROOMS

Following through your kitchen style and colour scheme with co-ordinating decorated objects and accessories makes even a mass-produced or standard kitchen look more personal and interesting. Repeating patterns and shades onto hand-painted china is a simple way to achieve overall design integration to the room. And painting your own pieces is much easier and cheaper than shopping for complementary tiles, crockery and other items.

The options for designer china in kitchens and dining rooms are limitless — perhaps decorated china services; border floor and wall tiles; splashbacks; fruit bowls; platters and dishes; jugs, bowls and creamers; and storage jars and containers for flour, sugar, pasta, herbs and spices.

Splashbacks can be decorated with ceramic paints. A continuous, unbroken flow of decorative tiles over surfaces and walls creates a unified, spacious appearance. If a tiled surface is going to be used a lot for food preparation, confine a decorative motif or border to the outer row of tiles, since it is less likely to suffer wear and tear.

Many kitchens are tiled from the counter top to a row of cupboards above. You can paint a decorative

These hand-painted storage jars are a practical and beautiful addition to any kitchen. Based on yellow, blue, green, red and white, the jars are variations on the spice jar project on page 76. Cut the central shapes out of masking paper, and use as templates to paint around on the jar. Once dry, lift off the tape and decorate as required.

border along the top row of tiles, just under the cupboards, where there is little danger of abrasion. To give it more impact, you can alternate plain brightly coloured and white tiles in two rows along the top, and decorate the alternating white tiles with patterns.

Motifs and designs based on raw ingredients or finished recipes are always appropriate in a kitchen. You could paint big bowls of fruit, or realistic or stylized glass bottles of preserved fruits and vegetables at regular intervals along a tiled wall, just above counter height, or as a frieze near the ceiling. As a smaller-scale project, paint a different fruit or vegetable on every alternating tile, chequerboard fashion. The culinary motif can obviously extend to three-dimensional objects, such as bowls and plates.

Hang a row of decorated ceramic plates at regular intervals in the awkward space between the tops of cupboards and the ceiling, or use that space to display a collection of decorated ceramic jugs or bowls. The brighter the colours and bolder the design, the more impact they will have, given the height and distance from the viewer.

If you are confident of your artistic skills, you could do a life-sized, *trompe l'oeil* mural of ingredients, as they would appear in a country kitchen, on a large, blank rectangular area of white tiles above a counter. (Do a sketch scheme first, then scale it up to the correct size.) Perhaps paint a horizontal wooden beam with hooks, from which could hang painted ducks, pheasants and other wildfowl; ropes of onions, garlic or red chilli peppers; and salamis or other preserved sausages. Perhaps beneath these, as if standing on the counter,

Wall tiles with a simplified pansy motif make a delightful backdrop for this charming, purely decorative tea set (above left). The tiny pansies painted on the teapot (above) set the colour scheme for the sugar bowl and cups and saucers which, with their solid blocks of colour, could not be easier to paint. Interest comes from the bold combination of colours: the green saucer, the purple bowl, the yellow lid and green knob of the sugar bowl; and the purple handle of the yellow cup and saucer. You could, if wished, paint a few pansies, here and there, on the yellow ground, or scattered on the surface of the cup.

To create, draw or trace a suitable image and enlarge or reduce it to the size required. Transfer to the china (see page 150) and paint.

depict big baskets of fresh bread, heaped plates of fruit and vegetables, even bottles of wine. Such murals often featured in Victorian butchers' shops, and they can be effective, even when quite simple.

Kitchen floors receive heavy wear, but you could make a single row of tiles around the base of the wall, forming the equivalent of a skirting board or baseboard, and paint a low-level pattern such as black and white checks.

Decorate food storage jars with pictures of the contents: stylized pasta for pasta jars, wheat ears for flour, and so on. Use stencils or freehand lettering to label them. Decorate fruit bowls with individual types of fruit: wide, shallow bowls with a strawberry or grape motif, for example. An autumnal nut bowl could be decorated with a motif of overlapping, richly coloured autumn leaves, or even stylized squirrels. Decorate a coffee pot and set of mugs in co-ordinated colours and patterns (do a few extra mugs and store them, in case of breakages later). If you plan to use them for everyday use, keep the design well away from the rims for complete safety. The same can be done for a teapot, cups and saucers. Any of the crockery listed in 'Working with Ceramics' on page 136 would be suitable.

A good beginner's project would be a large, single-tile teapot stand, perhaps with a matching tea set to follow, as confidence is built up. Victorian tile teapot stands or trivets were manufactured with ceramic feet, but you could make a simple wire frame for yours. Another original and simple idea is to buy and decorate a set of china-handled cutlery, personalizing them with simple motifs.

In a dining room, a cluster of decorated plates makes a good focal point when hung on a wall, while a huge bowl decorated on the outside in the same colours and style could serve as a table centrepiece, perhaps filled with fruit, or flowers in toning colours. Glass-fronted 'breakfronts' are features of many American dining rooms, and can contain a collection of decorative designer china. The table-like surface of buffet sideboards can also be used to display hand-painted ceramics, such as decorative china candleholders and painted vases filled with fresh flowers.

Always follow paint manufacturers' instructions, guidelines and warnings about the use of ceramic paints in conjunction with food. Water- and solvent-based ceramic paints should not come in contact with food or the mouth, nor should vitrified enamel or any other paints containing lead or cadmium. If in doubt, contact the manufacturers. Bowls, plates, dishes and platters decorated with ceramic paints are for decorative use only, or for food such as wrapped boiled sweets, bananas or oranges, that have a natural or manufactured protective coating. You can adapt designs easily so that the objects can be used for serving or storing food. Storage jars, for example, can be decorated on the outer surface only, and bowls, jugs and mugs can have borders round the base alone.

Small orange diamonds, as intense and cheerful as pot marigolds, enliven the rich blue and fresh green of this unusual tea caddy. If you enjoy a variety of herbal teas, you've got the perfect excuse for a collection of tea caddies, each with the specific plant name on the label. See the project on page 76 and adapt it to this design; transfer the drawn design to the jar with carbon paper and then paint.

LIVING ROOMS AND HALLS

The living room is full of potential as a display area for decorated ceramic objects: tea sets, vases or fruit bowls can enhance coffee tables, shelves, bookcases and glass cabinets. Bookcases filled with books alone can look dull, but are easily enlivened by including the occasional designer ceramic object.

Room dividers often mark the transition from living to dining room in small apartments or houses. A collection of hand-painted ceramics on the glass shelves of a room divider can appear to float in space, allowing the objects to be appreciated from every angle. Glass shelves against a white wall have much the same effect, but are doubly effective in displaying ceramic objects, especially vases and pitchers, when against a mirrored wall. Even if you can't see the decoration in detail, the hint of a second row of objects behind the first adds a sense of depth and richness.

Living rooms and dining rooms in older houses sometimes feature alcoves. These, with hidden lighting and shelves, can be ideal for displaying a collection of hand-decorated ceramics. A tiled alcove could feature a mural of a hanging basket of stylized flowers and foliage. You could take it one step further; by painting a window frame and glazing bars, and perhaps a distant landscape, you could create the effect of a sunny window, especially if concealed lighting is used.

Fireplaces, once the only source of heat in a house, are now generally found only in living rooms. They are often the focal point of a room, and the mantelpiece is the natural choice for displaying a prized piece or collection of hand-painted ceramics, including candleholders and vases. Mirrors are traditional above mantelpieces, and a ceramic-framed mirror, painted in the colours of the interior decor, would add a distinctive co-ordinating finishing touch. In a non-working fireplace, whether permanently or just for the summer, one large ceramic plate in bright or pastel colours could counteract the 'black-hole' quality of an empty grate.

Tiled fireplace surrounds were popular in Victorian and Edwardian times, and though they suffered a period of ignominy and were ruthlessly ripped out, they are now back in favour. There are many permutations of tiled fireplaces, from the familiar tile-register fireplace, with tiles fixed in a cast-iron framework, to fireplace 'slabs', with tiles fixed to bases in a factory and then cemented into position as a complete surround to a free-standing central grate. Tiles can extend out, to form a hearth, and up

Clovers and tiny berries are the decorative motif on this hand-painted ceramic fireplace surround, colour co-ordinated to match the decor. For ceramic fireplace tiles, such as these, with a slightly raised, bas-relief design, use the same method as for the jug and plate on page 72.

A hand-painted china bowl could hold dried or fresh flowers, pot-pourri, or knick-knacks. This elegant blue and white pattern (see page 80 for project) would suit most living room decors.

to form a decorative horizontal backing to shelves on either side. An Art Nouveau motif of flowers, slender stems and twisted leaves would be ideal for decorating plain vertical tiles in a tile-register fireplace, both in terms of the surface shape available and (approximate) historical appropriateness.

Some nineteenth-century living and dining room furniture featured built-in tiles on chair backs, table surfaces, stools, sideboards and cupboards. It is unlikely that you could find such pieces with plain white tiles, ready for painting, but you could buy a stripped pine equivalent, then tile and decorate it. Trunks and chests also provide excellent surfaces for applying hand-decorated tiles.

Ceramic lamp bases offer large-scale opportunities for decorative paintwork, automatically highlighted whenever the light is on. The decorative pattern on a lampshade could be repeated on the base, or the colours picked out in a simplified motif.

Purely ornamental are realistic or mythological animal sculptures in terracotta or with a white glaze, and in various sizes. Paint them either in lifelike or stylized colours: a black and white spotted Dalmation, for example, a mythical blue and white Chinese Foo dog or just a marmalade or calico cat. Small animal sculptures can sit on a coffee table; large, floor-standing types could guard the entrance to a living room, or lurk in the foliage in a conservatory.

Victorian tile manufacturers produced large, beautifully decorated tiles which were collected and displayed, even framed as pictures. You could do a decorative pattern or even a 'proper' painting, such as a tiny landscape, on a tile and frame it. Such tiles would make lovely presents, and could be hung in virtually any room of the house.

Halls are usually narrow, small transitional spaces, not for cluttering up or lingering in. Nonetheless, there are a number of decorative possibilities: a mirror in a decorated, ceramic tile frame or mosaic frame, made of broken tiles, could create the illusion of doubled space; a painted ceramic umbrella stand could be pretty as well as practical; letters ready to post could sit on a decorated ceramic tray; and flowers could fill a decorated ceramic jug, or pot-pourri a decorated ceramic bowl – all painted in a style and colourway complementary to the 'look' of the room as a whole.

BEDROOMS

There are many possibilities for incorporating decorated china in a bedroom, the room which allows you the most scope for exploring personal taste and style. Vases, jugs, bowls, decorative chamber-pots, dressing table accessories, and so on, can be painted with individual designs or to tie in with the overall theme of the room, whether classic or country floral, blue and white, or vivid modernist pattern.

Ceramic tile surfaces are rare in bedrooms, since they are cold to the touch and also have a visual coolness, which is unsuitable in a room where warmth, at least in temperate climates, is desirable. Country and old-fashioned bedrooms are often furnished with period wooden wash-stands, with tiled tops. Though

These decorative plates, sugar bowl and lamp base make an attractive display on a sideboard or occasional table in a living room. The lamp has been painted in typical Art Deco colours and pattern, with geometric, stylized roses. It was inspired by the genuine Deco squared-off plate shown.

ready-decorated tiles were often used, you could make your own washstand by tiling and painting a small, upright scrubbed pine table.

Large china basins and jugs, often decorated with floral motifs, were once traditional bedroom equipment, and plain large, shallow bowls and jugs can be painted with an old-fashioned design or a startling and original one. You can paint them to match existing Victorian tiles on a washstand, or start afresh on a multiple project, painting tiles, basin and jug to match.

Ceramic-based bedside lamps can be decorated to repeat the patterns on the shade, wallpaper or even bedspread and, if space allows, a pretty matching pot-pourri-filled bowl could scent the room. White china dressing table accessories are ideal for decorating: china-backed hair or clothes brushes, china jewellery trays

and ring trees, and so on, repeating the colours of the wallpaper or curtains. Small, prettily shaped plain white china pots and bowls could be decorated and used to hold small pieces of jewellery, make-up or hair clips. Precious family photographs could even be displayed in colour-co-ordinated hand-painted or mosaic china frames.

BATHROOMS

Although the bathroom is often the last room to be looked at decoratively in a house, it offers scope for painted china. Embellishing a bathroom with decorated ceramics is an easy way to add interest and coherence to a room, and designs can be applied to all manner of surfaces: the outside of the bath itself; the washbasin; a washstand; the cistern; tilework; soap dishes; jugs; pots and holders of all kinds, can all be painted.

A hand-painted china doorknob and panel add a lovely, old-fashioned detail to a plain door. The examples shown are quite elaborate, with their clusters of fruit joined by leaves, but you could do a simpler design, with a simple, linear motif.

A collection of blue and white spongeware ceramics enlivens a bedside table. When displaying your hand-painted ceramics, don't hesitate to include other objects, such as this transfer-printed blue and white cup and saucer, that add to the overall effect. Other options would be dark blue Bristol glass or blue, semi-precious stone eggs or spheres.

Restrained diamond and garland motifs in blue and gold decorate an off-white bathroom jug. The eighteenth-century inspired design is elegant in its simplicity, and though the colour scheme is perfect for its blue and white setting, it could also be interpreted in black, dark green, russet or rich wine red and gold.

Painted tiles can look elegant and contribute to the overall look. Hand-decorating plain white tiles is an economical way to create the same opulent effect as expensive purchased ones. Ceramics and tiles that are going to get a lot of wear and tear in a bathroom, or splashed with water, need to be painted with care. Tiles can be painted and baked before being mounted, but more normally you will need to paint *in situ*. Follow the detailed instructions on page 141 for painting onto tiles, and seal all ceramic surfaces with several layers of polyurethane varnish to add gloss, if wished, and protection from water. A gentle wipe is all that is needed to keep them clean; avoid rubbing with abrasive cleaners.

In interior design terms, bathrooms are usually small and contain solid-coloured or white fittings, so specially decorated tiles will enhance or set off the decor rather than compete with other patterns. Many of the suggestions for decorative friezes given in the section on kitchens also apply to bathrooms. Individual tiles can be painted, or a larger mural. The former can be placed around the ceiling, or frame a shower stall door or the splashback area of a hand-basin. Especially effective for murals is a square or rectangle of white tiles set in darker tiles above a shower, hand-basin or sink and/or toilet. The white tiles become the 'canvas'; the darker tiles, the 'frame'. And with a bath set in tile surrounds, use the outer vertical surface as a mural, or do a border pattern around the edge.

Suitable aquatic motifs for a bathroom include waves, starfish, sailing boats, ducks and waterfowl. Children's bathrooms offer scope for whole seaside scenes, including lifeguards, beach umbrellas, buckets or pails and spades; or, alternatively, motifs based on dolphins, porpoises or penguins. A mural above the bath could depict Noah's ark, complete with pairs of animals.

But motifs needn't be aquatic. You could paint two Classical columns, one either side of the entrance to a shower or toilet alcove; a big, over-flowing basket of flowers on the tiled splashback behind the basin; or a row of hanging baskets along the top of the shower or bath alcove. You could hand-paint a small motif around the rim of a ceramic sink, especially attractive on reproduction Victorian ones, perhaps scattering tiny rosebuds outside the basin itself . . . Soap dishes can be decorated outside and inside with small-scale motifs.

You can repeat through a bathroom the design, as it is or in simplified form, of patterned shower curtains or towels. Remember, though, that you have to live with the ceramics long after you replace the towels or curtain!

CONSERVATORIES AND GARDEN ROOMS

Ceramics are ideal in conservatories and garden rooms since they are impervious to water and potting soil or compost.

Unglazed terracotta flowerpots and tubs can be painted, allowing large areas of terracotta colour to remain as

Ceramic painting can be subtle, too. This Italian terracotta pot, with its rose and garland relief motif, is enhanced by a pale yellow emulsion wash on the body of the pot, and yellow over dark green on the relief pattern. This technique is perfect for beginners, since you can't really go wrong, and it is good for adding instant patina to a new terracotta pot.

background; alternatively the whole outer surface and inner rim can be painted white or pastel and a geometric, floral or leafy motif added. Many ceramic and terracotta pots have optional, matching saucers; buy and paint both, for a unified appearance. Terracotta pots painted in a *faux* bamboo motif add a light, airy, tropical touch. Placed on inexpensive bamboo plant stands, they become instant jardinières. For extra height, you could decorate a second-hand terracotta or stoneware chimney pot and insert a flowerpot in the top.

Genuine period jardinières are very expensive, but you could buy a cheap, white glazed reproduction, and paint it with rich colours and patterns. A simple, white-glazed chamber-pot could be decorated and placed on a wrought-iron plant stand base, perhaps painted to match. A reproduction tiered wirework fern stand could hold dozens of small, hand-decorated pots, with a unified colour theme but variations on a pattern. On a smaller scale, an old-fashioned tiered kitchen pot stand could hold three or four decorated pots; largest at the bottom, smallest at the top.

Terracotta floor tiles can be decorated with stencilled border motifs, with all-over patterns or with a central, carpet-like area of rich decoration. Remember, though, that painted floor

This chest is based on the same principles and techniques as the tile-covered window box on page 128, and makes a lovely conservatory hold-all. It could also be the centrepiece for a vignette of blue and white, hand-painted ceramics.

tiles can be scratched by pots, and excess water, laden with salts from the potting soil or compost and leaking from the drainage holes, can discolour ceramics and paint alike.

Large areas of tiled wall are ideal for decorating with floral murals, since conservatories and garden rooms can look bare in winter, and painted motifs can provide a permanent, leafy and flowery background. A stylized or *trompe l'oeil* flowering or fruiting tree, complete with flowerpot; or climbers such as grape vines, roses or passion flowers, could be painted. A refinement could be using black and white, or green and white, lattice-patterned tiles to represent a trellis over which a climber could be painted. *Trompe l'oeil* tropical birds, nestling among branches or in gilded or bamboo cages, could be added, or flitting butterflies or dragonflies. Bear in mind that fiercely bright green can make the colour of real foliage look dull by comparison, and spoil the appreciation of the variation in natural foliage colour, so try to use a subdued or dark green, instead, perhaps with bright green highlights.

A painted tile-topped chest can make an attractive and practical serving or display table. Tiny bedside tables could be tiled on top, hand-decorated and painted in toning colours, to make unusual plant stands.

Some conservatories have small, built-in ornamental pools which could be embellished with a tiled edge, with a floral motif or simple sponged or stippled texture, using perhaps a pale grey to soften the bright turquoise of traditional pool tiles.

PATHS AND PATIOS

All the suggestions given above for ceramic and terracotta pots and saucers can also apply to planters and pots within sheltered patios. Ceramic and bisque paints adhere well to terracotta; apply bisque stain quite thickly as pottery is porous. Polyurethane varnish or ceramic spray sealant will protect the pieces from the weather.

You could edge a brick or stone patio in hand-decorated tiles, inset into ordinary bricks or pre-cast concrete slabs. You can hand-paint your house's name or number on a large tile or ceramic plaque, and build it into the brickwork of the house or garden wall, or fix it onto an existing wall. Quarry-tile steps can have delicate border patterns painted on the risers. Flower boxes could be tiled front and sides with hand-decorated tiles, perpetuating a popular nineteenth-century tradition.

The sunny yellows and fresh greens of a spring garden are ideal inspiration for a set of painted terracotta flowerpots. Simple patterns and all-over colour washes are best, since they stand out well against the large scale of a garden setting. If you have the pots, paints and storage space, you could do several sets of pots, each set in a different colourway.

CREATING A STYLE

The advantage of designing your own hand-painted ceramics is not only the thrill of creating something beautiful and unique, but the possibilities it opens up in interior design. You can choose tones, details and patterns to reflect your personal taste, and to complement the colour scheme and style of the room.

When designing your decoration, consider the purpose of the object and its setting, whether for everyday use in a rustic kitchen, or for display in a sophisticated living room. Try to respond to the decor of the room, whether based on floral patterns and shades of rose and blue, or bright Mediterranean shades such as turquoise and Etruscan red. Simple gradations of a single colour can create an attractive effect; an intricate figurative design, another. Whatever you choose, even a single piece of hand-decorated china can make a strong statement, adding instant colour and life to a room.

Ceramics can be painted to fit in exactly with a chosen style. As dazzling as a Mediterranean summer, this geranium-filled window box (right) features hand-painted tiles in Portuguese colours of blue and yellow, with acid green and yellow painted terracotta pots nearby. The Medieval-style plate (above) would suit both a traditional and starkly modern interior (see projects on page 128 and 124).

CHOOSING A STYLE

Use hand-painted ceramics to enhance and emphasize the existing style of a room, as the starting point for creating a new decorative style, or simply to add colour and interest to the ordinary mix of things that, for most people, is 'home'.

'Style' refers to those visual characteristics that, together, make up a particular type of artistic expression or decorative method. Like inspiration, a style can be historical, based on a specific period in your own or another country's past; or contemporary, reflecting the latest interior design fashion. Style can be ethnic, inspired by a specific culture's use of colour and pattern, such as Mediterranean or Mexican style.

Most important of all, style can be personal. Many people have homes decorated in an eclectic way, a visual patchwork made up of elements of various styles or no particular style. This is sometimes a result of necessity: when setting up home on a shoestring budget for example, or inheriting family furniture. It can also be a conscious decision, since a meticulously correct and detailed room in one specific style can have the cold, anonymous feeling of a movie set or showroom, especially if the style is far

removed, in time or place, from the local idiom. Then, too, many people feel that they want to express their own personal style to the full, mixing and matching elements that they find appealing, whatever their origin.

Some historical styles are themselves eclectic. The Victorian style, especially High Victorian, is a virtual battleground of various styles: Greek Revival, Roman Revival, Gothic Revival, Venetian, Chinese, and others, all vying for attention in overstuffed rooms. And some ceramic styles have become so universally popular that they fit comfortably in a wide range of interior decors. Blue and white willow pattern, for example, which originated in England around 1780 and was based on earlier Oriental designs, is at home in Georgian, Regency, Victorian and Edwardian decors, as well as more humble but popular country cottage and farmhouse kitchen interiors.

Some motifs are common to many styles and cultures. The wave, or evolute spiral, motif, for example, occurs in Greek, Anglo-Saxon, Mexican and New Guinea decorative arts. Even the archetypal Greek fret or key pattern, made of continuous straight lines joined at right angles, also occurs in

These transfer-printed and majolica Victorian tiles and plate feature floral motifs. The special majolica technique of applying a semi-translucent coloured coating over an opaque white enamel base creates a lustrous glow, which you can partially recreate by applying a thin paint wash over white ceramic blanks.

The rich, deep colours and bold graphic forms of this Fifties- or Retro-style fruit bowl look even better in the company of fresh fruit. The variation in brushstrokes creates a translucent quality, as if the bowl were illuminated from within, a technique reminiscent of Victorian majolica.

Chinese, Mexican, Islamic and Fiji Island motifs, to just name a few.

While museums and antique shops may display domestic furniture and household effects going back hundreds of years to encompass Tudor, Stuart, Restoration and English Baroque styles, the majority of domestic decorations reflect the last 200 years.

When decorating ceramics in a particular style, it is more effective (and easier!) to attempt to capture its essence or feeling, rather than attempting to reproduce it exactly. By choosing a suitably shaped object and the correct palette of colours, you are more than half-way there before you even start. Getting the scale of the pattern correct – deciding whether it should be imposing or delicate, large or small – is the next hurdle, but the actual evolution of the pattern is where your creativity can come in.

On the following pages some classic and fashionable styles or 'looks' are described, and ideas given for creating co-ordinating designer china to complement these popular decors. Obviously, a room that is rigid in its design or theme can be a dull one, but the potential for following a style through with painted accessories is one of the most enjoyable aspects of decorative ceramics. To be able to design and create a complete room style from scratch is unusual – more often, a style has been built up gradually. Specially created china can bridge the gap, combining a number of design elements from the fabrics, furniture and accessories of a room, to give a more unified effect. A single

beautifully painted piece can help emphasize a room's style – a pretty floral vase gives a country cottage feel; a more dramatic design in blue, orange and gold will give a Thirties look; a distressed terracotta and turquoise painted pot has a summery Mediterranean effect. Be inspired by and adapt the suggestions and descriptions that follow to create painted china to suit your own favourite style.

CLASSICAL STYLE

'Classical', in the narrow sense, means the architectural or decorative motifs of ancient Rome or Greece. Today, 'Classical' refers more generally to any style that is closely or loosely based on these motifs, and is formal, often symmetrical, and timeless in its appeal. Classical can be simple and restrained, as in early Georgian and Colonial American styles, or frivolous, as in Baroque, Rococo and Regency styles.

A plain room can be given instant antique elegance with a large, striking urn painted with Etruscan colours, or Greek-style black figures on a dull red background. You could adapt Classical motifs such as the column and use them in a modern monochromatic scheme for a highly stylized effect. Laurel wreaths, once used to crown the heads of emperors, are an obvious Classical symbol, and can be depicted in stencilled or hand-painted forms. Fruit and flower swags, 'egg and dart' pattern friezes, Classical urns and griffins, as favoured by Robert Adam, the great English Georgian architect, can be stencilled on tile walls, or hand-painted round jugs, pots, vases and teapots.

Acanthus leaves, deeply lobed and almost sculptural in form, are another instantly recognized Classical motif, and a single row of leaves can enhance a simple jug, vase or frieze.

Cameo-style, side-view silhouettes are also Classical in feeling, especially set against an oval ground of soft colour, such as coral, grey or Wedgwood blue. It might be fun to do a series of family portraits this way, one per decorative plate, and hang them clustered on a wall.

Suitable colours include grey-green; cream and peach; rich, dark green with gold and bronze; and touches of white and gold to add liveliness to any of the above. Avoid sugary pastels by adding a bit of brown or grey to the tint. American Colonial-style motifs are largely simplified, natural renderings of fruit and flowers, and are best depicted in earthy reds, dull greens, soft browns and dark blue-greys.

Stylized acanthus leaves, vine leaves and grapes are easily copied or adapted for decorating ceramics in the Classical style. The Greek key pattern, however, with its rigidly parallel lines, demands a steady hand and much practice! Black, white and terracotta, and simple, especially symmetrical, shapes, such as the double-handled urn, also have strong Classical overtones.

As decorative on a shelf as they are on a dining table, these verdigris-painted Classical candleholders will have a strong impact on any mantelpiece or dining table (see page 154 for painting techniques).

Cherubs and tassels are more light-hearted Classical images, as is *trompe l'oeil*, a popular device of seventeenth- and eighteenth-century artists in which startlingly realistic-looking, three-dimensional still lifes were painted. Rococo decorative motifs, such as fantastic scrolls and shell images, are light, curvilinear and elegant; colours are equally light-hearted, with pastel tints predominating, such as lilac, lavender and peach.

The Classical also has its humorous side; the early nineteenth-century French Empire period, during Napoleon's reign, favoured hot-air balloons as motifs in honour of the Montgolfier brothers, who ascended in the first hot-air balloon; deep purple, pale lilac, azure blue, deep green, rich ochre, and strong, stinging yellows, are typical 'Empire' colours, and marble and tortoiseshell, typical of the period, are easily reproduced textural effects.

Regency style, named after the English Prince Regent in the early nineteenth century and exemplified by the splendid confusion of styles in The

Royal Pavilion, Brighton, features sophisticated combinations of strong colours: crimson and emerald green; sulphur yellow and lilac; and strong blue, dark pink and gold. Coalport china, with its panels of delicately painted fruit, flowers and birds, is a good reference for inspiration if your artistic skills are well developed, but Regency style is also known for its stripes and simple stencilled friezes, often in Greek key patterns, and you could use these themes on ceramic objects in the colours listed above. Regency also encompasses Egyptian, Gothick and heavily gilded Chinoiserie styles, the latter with exotic flowers, birds and Oriental figures and landscapes. False, or *faux*, bamboo was another favourite device.

VICTORIAN STYLE

The Victorian period, from 1837 to 1901 is, like Regency, an 'umbrella' term covering a plethora of styles, often combined in muddled unison. Victorians looked to the past for inspiration, and borrowed ideas from Classical, Medieval Romanesque and Gothic periods, as well as the more exotic Egyptian, Persian and Oriental sources. Heavy, ornate decoration, machined rather than hand-crafted, as exemplified by the Great Exhibition of 1851 in Hyde Park, London, is what most people think of as Victorian. Almost any subject and pattern was (and is) fair game for Victorian decorative ceramic motifs, from idealized romantic pastoral or biblical scenes to tartan plaids, the latter a result of Queen Victoria's acquisition

of Balmoral Castle and subsequent love of all things Scottish.

The Victorians were fascinated by nature, both from a scientific and romantic point of view. Garden flowers, together with wild and exotic plants and animals, are all suitable motifs, and can be painted in realistic or interpretive style. Flowers and arabesques were common motifs on wallpaper, especially the new, cheap wallpapers produced on rotating cylinders rather than by block-printing, and these patterns make very effective designs for 'period' pots, vases and tiles. Many of the modest, country-cottage styles, such as scattered rose-buds on a plain ground, are easy to repeat with ceramic paints. Huge floral bouquets are another common motif, but many of these original ceramic motifs were done by transfer printing, which enabled a much greater degree of detail and realism than is sensibly attempted in hand-painting.

Domestic interiors were often painted sombre colours, such as terracotta, deep green or Etruscan brown, but virulent colours from chemical dyes also first appeared in Victorian times. They included acid yellow, brilliant crimson, saturated bright blue and fierce greens, and were popularly used in fabric and carpet manufacture. The many Medieval-style tile designs produced by Thomas Minton in conjunction with Augustus Pugin used simple geometric patterns in sombre, rich colours — rusty red, terracotta, indigo blue, Prussian blue and deep brown —

The 'Victorian' style is really a collection of many different styles, but features floral designs strongly; exotic, garden and wild flowers provided inspiration for hand-painted and transfer-printed ceramics, on white, as shown, and on coloured backgrounds. Pansies, with their rich colour range, infinite variations and charming 'faces' were special favourites.

enlivened with touches of gold, yellow or black outlines. They make ideal inspiration for Victorian-style ceramics and tiles.

Victorian ceramic vases and other objects were often ornately shaped, perhaps more to show the skill of the manufacturer than to create a beautiful object. Today, these ornate shapes are out of favour, but some Victorian ceramic manufacturers, such as Wedgwood, also created white- or cream-glazed ceramics of timeless simplicity, and reproductions of these are excellent bases for Victorian-style ceramic decoration.

Displaying collections of china is as Victorian as the china itself, whether elaborate tea services or purely ornamental objects and knick-knacks. You need not aim for the overcrowded, hectic effect of High Victorian interior style, but a carefully composed grouping of hand-painted ceramics can add a nice Victorian touch. Or, in keeping with the Victorian penchant for china mementoes from seaside holidays, you could paint holiday scenes on a series of little jugs, teacups and saucers or plates.

Of all the styles of the Victorian period, the one most suitable for ceramic decoration is that of the Arts and Crafts Movement. Natural plant dye colourings influenced the palette, used in the paintings of Rossetti, Whistler and Burne-Jones, of burgundy, plum red, hyacinth blue, purple, soft dusky green or deep forest green, pale lemon yellow, medium blue and old rose pink, and neutral colours from white to cream to deep grey.

Medieval, Italian, Persian and Oriental ceramics and textiles provided inspiration, and natural sources, especially flowers, provided the main subject matter. Spurning the brightly coloured, realistic, densely packed bunches of exotic pelargoniums, fuchsias and rhododendrons depicted by most designers, William Morris concentrated on simplified, two-dimensional forms of native English hedgerow and garden plants such as jasmine, marigold, honeysuckle, daisy and crown imperial lily. Willow boughs and acanthus leaves served as foliage in his wallpaper and textile designs, used with the diamond- or ogee-patterned net, or the asymmetrical, meandering-branch framework of repeats. Another inspiring reference for Arts and Crafts ceramic patterns are the pottery and tiles of William de Morgan, of which there are some 300 designs.

Natural forms, especially flowers, appear in the decorative arts the world over, and range from Victorian realistic representations to highly derivative, stylized or simplified symbols. Recording flowers either photographically or freehand, in a sketchbook, helps you become familiar with their form and increases your visual awareness, whether or not you use that particular study in a design. Collecting objects decorated with a floral motif, from greeting cards and fabric samples to odd bits of china, is a good way to build up a reference library of floral images.

ART NOUVEAU STYLE

This lasted only from 1890 to 1900 but was a powerful influence on decorative arts. Art Nouveau designs can be based on elongated rectilinear forms and tight floral ornamentation, as in the work of Charles Rennie Mackintosh; or on elongated, flowing, sensuous, undulating lines, loosely taken from natural forms, as in the drawings of Aubrey Beardsley.

Flowers feature heavily, especially lilies, orchids, arum lilies, tulips, lotus, poppies and irises. Tiles in series often included four vertically aligned tiles depicting flowers with attenuated curving stems and leaves. Stylized birds, especially peacocks, are popular motifs.

Rich bands of stencilling are typical of Art Nouveau, as are brilliant lustre glazes. 'Tube lining' – raised seams of clay separating different areas of coloured glazes – was much used in ceramics. You can achieve the visual effect of this on a modern pot by applying a thin outline of black or other dark shade between areas of colour.

For a simple project in the Art Nouveau style, simply divide the surface to be painted into a series of interlocking, organic shapes, using undulating black lines. When dry, fill each space with a different colour, perhaps concentrating on watery blues, greens and mauves, or stained glass colours. Tall, slender ceramic objects, with elegantly curved silhouettes, are perfect for painting in an Art Nouveau style; inexpensive Oriental white china lotus bowls can, for instance, be painted with stylized lotuses, lilies or tulips.

Arum lilies, or zantedeschias, with their elegant, curvaceous shapes, provide the perfect inspiration for an Art Nouveau decorative motif. Long-stemmed lilies, tulips, iris, lotus and poppies are equally suitable, and if the ceramic is itself fluid and organic in shape, so much the better. Period colours range from the rich hues of Tiffany lamps to the subtle, watery tones of Lalique – the choice is yours.

MEDIEVAL STYLE

The Medieval era, or Middle Ages, lasted from the fifth to the twelfth century A.D. The period brings to mind images of pageantry and chivalry — all the ingredients of legend and fairy tale. Although for the majority of people at that time life was in all probability unpleasant, the decorative motifs of this era are enchanting and appeal to modern-day eyes.

The two main Western European styles, which themselves varied from country to country, were first Romanesque and then Gothic. The Middle Ages ended with the Renaissance, but the Gothic tradition was kept alive, first by the eighteenth-century Gothick Revival, which was based on frothy, superficial Gothic-style decoration, and later by the more serious-minded nineteenth-century Gothic Revival, within which Gothic detailing was transformed by rich and glorious Victorian colours. The current fashion for 'Gothic' and 'Medieval' ornamentation, which is really a response to the rich jewel colours and striking motifs of the era, is much more easily achieved on the small-scale, two-dimensional plane of painted ceramics than it is with furniture or three-dimensional architectural detail. Simply by choosing the right paint colour and motif to paint, you can recreate the sombre splendour of these times in even the most anonymous modern 'box'-like room.

Medieval imagery, with its rich colours, forms and symbolic associations, holds a strong fascination today. Most universal is the fleur-de-lis, based on the iris flower, but simplified mythological and religious motifs, carefully observed flora and fauna and simple geometric patterns are equally Medieval, especially when interpreted in the rich colours of tapestries or heraldic hues, or the neutrals of old stone. For a project based on a Medieval theme, see page 124.

To reproduce this Medieval-style decorative china (see the project on page 124), use earthy colours such as warm yellow or red ochres, raw umber, raw or burnt sienna, and greens such as terre verde or sharp sap green. Or use stone-like greys, grey-greens, dusty beiges or tans; the rich colours of tapestries or damasks; or the bright colours of stained glass, illuminated manuscripts or heraldic devices.

Early Medieval patterns include a series of pointed arches, connected 'V' shapes or chevrons, and diapers, which are lozenges, diamonds, squares or more complicated shapes repeated continuously over a panel or wall surface. To reproduce them, use earthy colours such as warm yellow or red ochres, raw umber, raw or burnt sienna, and greens such as terre verde or sharp sap green. Or use stone-like greys, grey-greens, dusty beiges and tans; the rich colours of Medieval tapestries or damasks; or the bright colours of stained glass, illuminated manuscripts and heraldic devices. Heraldic colours include yellow, white, blue, red, green, black and violet, technically referred to as, respectively, 'or' (gold), 'argent' (silver), 'azure', 'gules', 'vert', 'sable' and 'purpure'. And even simple, freehand drawings in red ochre alone can capture the Medieval feeling.

Suitably Medieval subjects to adapt in your own designs could include biblical and traditional Christian symbolism − a lily, for example, was symbolic of Mary's purity − grotesques, which are fantastic combinations of human and animal forms, and stylized birds, fish and animals, flowers and trees. For borders depict, in simplified form, grape vines, interlocking ivy or oak leaves, rows of stylized 'ball' flowers − each flower within a circular outline − or 'tablet' flowers − each bloom filling a square frame. Period mouldings that can be copied two-dimensionally include the cross-like, diagonal dog-tooth patterns, and the billet, nail-head, double-cone, beak-head and cable patterns.

Motifs taken from heraldry, including the heraldic shield or *blazon* itself, are ideal; there are also the evocative unicorns, griffins, lions, dogs, crowns, fleur-de-lis and the simple Tudor rose. Every heraldic motif is symbolic: the boar, for instance, stands for cunning and ferocity; the swan, unicorn and white hart for purity and innocence; the lion for leadership; the tower for security, and keys refer to heaven and hell − you could use an image with its 'meaning' deliberately in mind, or purely for its visual impact.

On a lighthearted note, Medieval heraldic devices and mottoes were often based on puns on the family name, and you might try constructing your own 'coat of arms' in a similar way. There are books on heraldry that provide the full vocabulary.

AMERICAN COUNTRY STYLE

Informal, unpretentious, practical yet welcoming and modestly decorative, the traditional eighteenth- and nineteenth-century American country style is an ideal choice for creative ceramic painting.

Borders and all-over patterns are a typical feature of American country style. Colours are bold: black, white, Indian red, yellow ochre, and verdigris green. Patterns are equally bold: circles within squares, or diamond patterns, within which are simple floral and leaf motifs.

Use lines of tiles to divide large walls into smaller panels, and, should

As American as apple pie, this Colonial-style vase draws its inspiration from several sources, including nineteenth-century American stencils, with their child-like yet powerful simplicity; old wooden jigsaw toys; the reds and whites of crisp checked fabrics; and the mini-prints of modest wallpapers. The more visual references you have, the more effective your design is likely to be.

there be a mantelpiece, display in the area above it, or the 'overmantel', a single, large ceramic, such as a flower-filled urn. Motifs can range from a repeated single leaf, to stylized leaf and flower forms with bells, hearts, swags, foliage, fish and wave designs or, by contrast, geometric forms or ribbons. For strong colours, red, green, black and yellow are traditional, often applied onto pink, white, pale yellow, grey, light green or light blue plaster walls.

Decorated folk ceramics of the period take four traditional forms: sgraffito, in which a design is scratched through a thin, outer coating of clay to reveal a different colour clay beneath; slipware, in which liquid clay of one colour is poured from a special cup through hollow quills of various sizes onto a clay object of another colour; stoneware, hard, dense, salt-glazed clay usually decorated with cobalt blue designs; and the self-descriptive spongeware.

You can't recreate the exact effect of the Pennsylvania Dutch sgraffito and slip-decorated techniques with ceramic paints, but you can borrow their colours and feel: clay red, scratchy lines against a cream ground, for sgraffito; and a clay red ground with irregular, fluid, almost

bobbly lines of cream, for slipware. (You could achieve this effect on ceramics by painting the wiggly lines with masking fluid on your object, applying a flat background colour, then peeling off the masking fluid when dry.) The blue decorative motifs on New York State stoneware jugs and crocks have the feeling of relaxed, almost Oriental, quick pen-and-ink sketches; eagles, fish, deer, frogs, vases of flowers and other homely subjects were popular. Spongeware was usually blue and white, with an all-over texture or simple, geometric or stylized motifs.

Rural American motifs are wide-ranging in subject matter but tend to be primitive or naive in execution, without a hint of three-dimensional quality. American eagles and early American flags, symbols of American liberty, are appropriate, as are simple renditions of the paddle-wheel boats and clipper ships, ships' figureheads and other wooden carving of the time. Other subjects include the Tree of Life and bowls of fruit, with grapes, peaches, pears, cherries, blackberries, melons and pineapples, the last a symbol of hospitality. The animal world, angels and American Indians, sea serpents, even steam engines, served as inspiration for stencilling and hand-painted folk art. Traditional wooden waterfowl decoys are themselves simplified forms, and are ideal for interpreting in ceramic paints. Their simple, instantly 'readable' silhouettes are perfect for stencilling, whether onto a tile-covered box or on a tiled wall.

From Pennsylvania Dutch barns come painted decorations, or hex signs, in yellow, blue, red and green painted on a circular white ground. Some designs are based on the six-lobed tulip, others on a pomegranate.

Quilts, samplers, and stencilled cloths are infinitely rich sources of inspirational patterns. By repeating a single motif extracted from patterned fabric – a tiny spiral, sprig or trio of dots, for example – in horizontal or vertical stripes around a vase or jug, you create an object that combines the traditional, American country feel with a contemporary one, at home in either setting.

ENGLISH COUNTRY STYLE

English country houses range from castles and vast stately homes to modest cottages and, historically, from the Middle Ages to contemporary designs. Until the nineteenth century, building materials and style were almost always dictated by local availability and custom, and differed from one locale to another.

In popular interior design terms, however, the idea of the English country cottage, nestled in its flowery garden, and the Edwardian country house, with its generously proportioned rooms and luxurious hospitality, has caught the imagination – not only among the urban English, but all over the developed world, including, interestingly, Japan.

The country cottage style brings to mind an amalgam of periods: timeless stone, tile, brick or wood floors; scrubbed pine furniture, including

Inspiration for designs and colour schemes can be from eclectic sources – these Shaker-style template, with their strong, clearly delineated use of colour, would provide good reference for painting an authentic American Country pot.

the farmhouse dresser and wash-stand; Victorian sprigged floral curtains and wallpaper; a cheerful mixture of china patterns, both hand-painted and transfer-printed, especially the ubiquitous blue and white willow pattern; and collections of knick-knacks and modest, functional objects, such as jugs or wicker baskets, hung from beams or filling shelves. Patchwork quilts, a feature of American country homes of the time, feature here, too.

In an authentic 'English country cottage' decor, deliberately chosen, coherent colour schemes are irrelevant. Most colours come from the natural materials that make up the structure of the house and its furnishings, with sparks of lively colour provided by the smaller objects inherited or acquired, magpie fashion, over the generations. Unpremeditated, informal or even mildly disordered, practical and modest:

these are the hallmarks of English country cottage style – it is an excuse, when decorating ceramics, to use a variety of images and motifs.

The English Edwardian country house style is altogether more opulent, premeditated, leisurely and larger-scale. The small, country cottage jug filled with wild flowers or seasonal garden flowers is replaced by formal vases full of lavish displays of forced lilies and lilac and other hot-house flowers, welcoming but also impressive. Small-sprigged floral patterns give way to exuberant floral chintzes, with full-blown, larger-than-life roses and more exotic blooms, and references to Classical style appear. Decorative china plays a significant role in the displays of busy collections of china, framed photographs and *objets d'art*; but tends to be of a more conspicuous, deliberately chosen and carefully arranged nature than country cottage style.

A medley of china patterns based on roses, from delicate buds to sumptuous, full-blown blooms. Roses, like most flowers, can be interpreted in a number of styles, from the curved brushstrokes of English canalware and nineteenth-century American toleware, to larger-than-life Edwardian rose-patterned chintzes and mini-sprigged, English cottage garden blooms.

With its simple, functional forms, contemporary ethnic Mediterranean pottery often displays more than a hint of its Classical heritage. The subject matter – stylized fruits, especially grapes and foliage – also goes back thousands of years. The clear blue, yellow and green on a white ground and loose, freehand style are typical.

If you grow and dry your own herbs, what nicer way to store them than in your own, hand-painted, Provençal-style jars? Featuring a red as sharp and fiery as its contents, this chilli storage jar is a variation of the project on page 76.

MEDITERRANEAN STYLE

The uninhibited use of colour — whether clear, pure hues, subtly rich, earthy ones or colour-washed pastels – and simple, unpretentious decorative motifs, are the hallmarks of Mediterranean ceramic style. Craftsmanship and ornamentation are powerful, bold and solid, and tend more toward the crude than the refined, an approach also reflected in Mediterranean fabrics, furniture and, on a larger scale, architecture.

The ceramics of the Mediterranean are primarily functional. Non-matching china and kitchenware are an extension of the informal living style, and immensely practical, since replacements can be made without effort. (On the aesthetic front, it allows for endless pattern variations on a single-colour theme or closely related colours.)

There are traditional elements associated with Mediterranean style that have been taken up in more contemporary fashion; elements which have inspired adaptations that capture its essence – colour, light, and simplicity. Tiled floors are traditional: cool underfoot, simple to clean, timeless in feeling and almost timeless in durability, easily making the transition from the courtyard to the indoors and out again. In the Mediterranean tiles are used not only on walls and floors but to decorate window boxes, chests and plant holders, and these are projects perhaps more suited in scale to someone new to ceramic painting.

The typical rough white plasterwork wall is a result of the rougher stonework beneath as much as the plasterer's skills and traditions, and contrasts well with hand-painted, wall-hung ceramics. Deep niches in thick walls and deep windowsills can frame a group of ceramics, or a single, impressive piece. Open shelves, rather than built-in, concealed storage, are another Mediterranean feature and are a good 'excuse' for the display of ceramics.

The bright, sunny yellow of Portuguese and Spanish pottery makes a good base for a simple green glaze, applied in drips or as elementally simple motifs. Blue and white, especially the so-called Mediterranean blue, a clear, mid-tint, is another suitable combination; blue and white pictorial tiles are just one example. The red clay of the Mediterranean, used fully glazed or glazed on the inside only, is always comfortable and warm looking, the warmth of which is somehow retained even when opaque glazes are used.

Because the kitchen often has the dual role of living room, because the preparation, cooking and eating of food are of prime importance to the Mediterranean way of life, and because meals are long and lingering, kitchenware should reflect that weighting. It should also reflect the hearty simplicity of the Mediterranean cuisine.

Particularly French-Provençal is china with angled sides, such as octagonal-sided white china, but hand-moulded plates and hand-thrown jugs and bowls, with their uneven thickness, wholesome chunkiness and mild asymmetry, capture the flavour of the Mediterranean more than manufactured equivalents.

RETRO AND ART DECO STYLE

'Retro', from the prefix meaning 'backwards' or 'back again' has come to refer to fashions revived from the not-too-distant past, say, the Twenties, on. You can still find Retro ceramics in junk shops, though some famous ceramic designers/painters, such as Susie Cooper and Clarice Cliff, are now cult figures; their ceramics are museum pieces and change hands at vast prices.

For a Twenties style, use favoured combinations of bright orange, yellow, purple and fresh green, perhaps with a band of colour, varying from narrow to wide, around the rim or lip. Tulips; crocuses; hollyhocks; little cottage-garden land-scapes; delphiniums; and elongated, cartoon-like trees, with a hint of landscape behind, including cartoon-like cottages and

Although spanning only a brief period of twentieth-century design history, Art Deco has captured the hearts and imaginations of many devotees. Squat, chunky ceramics and strident colours, especially orange, yellow, purple and sharp green, on a cream – rarely white – background are easily adapted Deco hallmarks. Stylized crocuses, leaves, little cartoon-like landscapes, and geometry, especially sunburst patterns, are typical motifs. Obvious-looking brushstrokes are a feature, so you can relax when painting in the Deco style!

mountains, are suitable motifs. Fine-lined motifs of garlands of bay leaves, with oranges or bright red apples at regular intervals, are also authentically Twenties-style. Typical Twenties ceramic shapes are simple, straightforward and geometric, often squat and round, with prominent handles on lids; Clarice Cliff's famous 'Bizarre' range is archetypal.

In the Thirties, stylized antelopes and deer, simple polka dots in bright red or blue on a white ground, and stylized oak leaves painted at regular intervals over white ground, interspersed with small dots or diagonally angled around a plate rim, are typical. Stick ring-binder reinforcers randomly over a ceramic object, and colour-wash over it. When dry, carefully remove the stickers and you will have crisp, white rings against the background colour of your choice. Alternatively, use the stickers as a stencil, painting the inner circle for a small, solid and geometrically perfect dot. Semi-circular, overlapping paint strokes around the rim of a plate, with a stylized central floral motif, are also typical, as are concentric bands of varying thicknesses and colours, or 'wash-banding', with colour combinations such as grey, blue and green; or grey, brown and purple. A variation is concentric circles of narrow black or silver lines, half of each circle with undulating lines, the other half plain. Ceramics of the Thirties are simple and practical, with fluid, streamlined silhouettes. Asymmetry is a strong feature of Thirties and Forties ceramics, such as flowers painted diagonally across a plate; in the late Forties, simple banding was the only ceramic decoration featured during the post-War years in Britain.

Art Deco is a specific Twenties and Thirties style that is now enjoying a revival. Based on geometric, formalized design, it is derived from Egyptian and Mayan motifs, Cubism and Futurism. Colours, often with a slight lustre, are influenced by Post-Impressionist art, especially the Fauves, and range from neutral oatmeal, buff, beige and coffee to eau-de-Nil, pastel pink, peach, lilac and blue; and rich hues, such as deep ultramarine, red, dark green, orange, purple, dark brown and black. Typical colour combinations include black or dark green with red; black and lilac, red or silver; blue and red; and gold and silver detail generally. Motifs include crosses, chevrons, zigzags, circles and stylized fish.

Art Deco hand-painted vases can be of rough stoneware as well as smooth ceramic. Use simple, oval vases, possibly with a small, lipped rim; variations include narrow, elongated necks and round vases with tiny, rimless central apertures. Painting a narrow freehand black line around a simple motif, such as fruit or geometric shapes, can create a 'retro' feel, especially of the Thirties, Forties and Fifties.

In the Fifties the Festival of Britain influenced ceramic design, and many patterns were based on shapes of crystal structures as seen through a high-powered microscope; the popular 'Festival' design is a series of

The strong colours of this Deco-style lamp – orange, red, green and brown – in fact work very well together. The white bordering is extremely effective, and is simply achieved by stencilling.

parallel lines punctuated at random intervals with dots of various colours surrounded by rings. Polka dots are also typical: blue polka dots on a white teapot lid, for example, with a solid blue pot. Enlarged weaving patterns of horizontal and vertical painted black lines are enlivened with a second colour, such as red or yellow. Use bright, primary, optimistic and jazzy colours, with a touch of the Scandinavian – clean lines and form.

For a Sixties look, go for patterns based on Op Art, with black and white, sophisticated optical illusion; or 'flower power', with stylized daisies in psychedelic colours, such as lime green, purple, orange, and hot pink.

CHRISTMAS AND SPECIAL THEMES

The versatility of hand-decorated ceramics means that customized china can be created for all kinds of traditional occasions, and personal celebrations. Paint china specially for use at Christmas, Easter, Hallowe'en, Thanksgiving and other seasonal events; and with specific people in mind for individualized presents as well as for use on anniversaries.

At Christmas, plain, solid red or green ceramics are festive, especially if used on a contrasting red or green tablecloth, but a specific holiday motif makes them even more special. Holly and ivy leaves, either hand-painted or stencilled, embody the festive season, especially when enlivened

This pair of deep green and rich red marbled candleholders adds a festive Christmas note. Start with the solid red and green undercoat, then allow to dry and sponge with darker red or green. The white cracks are achieved with a feather and white paint. See page 155 for details. Sprigs of fresh ivy and dark green natural-fibre ribbon link the colour scheme into the room decoration.

As traditional as they are charming, these tartan-patterned plates in red, green and black would enliven any Christmas scene. For the rigid, right-angled effect, use strips of masking tape to work against and start with the broad, horizontal stripes (draw in the vertical stripes). For added effect, paint the cross-over squares in a darker shade. The narrow black lines are hand-painted.

by bright red holly berries. Large areas of sharp, acid greens are visually incompatible with the presentation of food, but in small amounts, however, they can enliven a dark green. For table crockery and vases, choose a rich forest green, which is closer to the deep tones of holly and ivy anyway. If you are hand-painting, use fresh ivy and holly as reference. You could encircle the rim with long trails of intertwined ivy leaves, as seen in some Victorian china patterns.

Stylized Christmas trees, a large one in the centre of a plate or dish, smaller ones round the edge, are

effective. A cylindrical vase could be decorated with one or more rows of connected Christmas trees, rather like paper doll cut-outs, perhaps with a few metallic baubles. A repeat pattern of stylized wrapped Christmas presents, perhaps with intertwined ribbon bows linking the packages, is another possibility. Huge, painted ribbon bows would be especially effective with square or rectangular serving plates, but you could paint a ribbon bow decoration around the rim of a bright red cylindrical vase. Christmas stockings, reindeer, bells, prettily wrapped presents, or stars in mixed

Christmas red and green has been painted onto ceramic candleholders; the painted 'marble' texture is easily achieved (see page 155).

metallic colours, including gold, silver, bronze and copper, could be stencilled or hand-painted on red or green plates. A traditional Christmas wreath, in holly or mixed conifer branches, is ideal for painting round the edge or rim of a plate or mug. Especially American are red and white striped candy canes, which can be clustered or repeated at regular intervals. If your skills allow, hand-painted sledges or sleighs, filled with presents, could decorate big platters.

Thanksgiving is as important in the American home as Christmas, and ceramics decorated with wild turkeys, ears of harvest corn, pumpkins and other gourds make the festival that much more special. For Easter, create a set of yellow- and blue-painted crockery, perhaps decorated with spring flowers or Easter themes: fluffy chicks, decorated eggs, and so on. A vase painted with yellow daffodils would be a wonderful centrepiece containing a bunch of the real thing.

CHILDREN'S CHINA

Children like bright, bold colours and simple images; for very young children, different coloured dots or, one step up from dots, balloons or kites on a sky-blue background, are cheerful and striking. Geometric designs, such as stripes, checks or as concentric rings of different colours, might echo the colour theme of a child's room.

Animals are great favourites with children, whether stylized jungle creatures, such as lions and giraffes, mythological creatures, such as the Loch Ness monster, or simple renditions of native wildlife, such as squirrels, rabbits or robins. Baby animals are especially endearing to children: fluffy baby bunnies, chicks, kittens or puppies. Perhaps a simple version of the family dog could decorate a plate or lamp base, with the lead encircling the rim. Children also like traditional characters from movies or story books, as well as the latest television or movie crazes.

Children's toys, with their bright colours and simple, easily identifiable shapes, are ideal source material for motifs for decorative plates and bowls. To paint this dish, see the project on page 106.

THE PROJECTS

On the following pages are step-by-step instructions for creating a whole range of different decorative china pieces, employing a wide range of techniques and styles. All the instructions you need to create the items shown are given, reinforced by easy-to-follow stage-by-stage photography; reference should also be made to the sections on basic materials, equipment and techniques on pages 134–155. However, all of the techniques and ideas shown can be easily adapted; a design and pattern from one project could be applied to a ceramic object other than that shown (see page 149 for instructions for working up a design), or you could apply your own design but use the same method. Colours can be changed to suit individual requirements of style, purpose and personal taste; illustrations of different colourways are included in many of the projects to indicate just some of the possibilities.

Display your collection of hand-painted china (right) with pride! Shelves, breakfronts or old-fashioned dressers in a living room, dining room, kitchen or hall can take on museum-like richness, as you gradually increase your skills and try new styles. There are projects here suitable for the beginner and the more advanced painter, from colour-washed garden pots to an intricate paisley teapot (above).

LOW-RELIEF JUG

Ceramics with low-relief decorative motifs are ideal for beginners to paint. Like children's colouring books, the shapes are all set out for you to colour in, and as there are no clearly defined outlines, minor mistakes are not noticeable. Reproduction Victorian white relief pattern jugs and creamware, and contemporary Portuguese white pottery, are all ideal.

This pattern, with its lemons and leaves, is an easy one to colour. In more complex patterns, you must work out in advance what you are going to emphasize, whether fruit, flowers, cherubs and so on, and how you are going to treat the secondary motifs, such as the leaves surrounding the lemons.

The rim has a slight edge which you can use as guidance when painting it, but if you are nervous about keeping a steady hand, omit the rim detail. If you are planning to use the jug for pouring drinks or storing milk, leave the rim blank; you could paint the handle bright yellow instead.

If you want to try painting on a plate rim similar to that shown, paint the berries and leaves first, then mask out the centre and paint the yellow ground and, finally, the rim.

A thin white rim is left around the edge of each colour. If you want these shades to join, however, then the object will need to be baked after each colour stage.

The white-on-white jug and plate shown are non-matching, but the use of yellows and greens, with a little red on the plate, creates a unified theme. The fruit and foliage motifs can be coloured naturalistically, as here, or to go with a particular decor; fabric colour combinations make a good starting point. Golden and rusty autumnal leaf tones would make a nice alternative to the green; the red berries on the plates could be treated as purple grapes; or both objects could be done entirely in black and shades of grey. You could use two colours only, one on the basic relief and the other on the base, or you could simply colour the background in a solid tone, such as Wedgwood blue, leaving the motif white, as in Victorian jasperware. Other options include painting the centre of the plate and body of the jug a solid colour, and dotting lemons or leaves over the body of the jug.

Tools and materials

White-glazed, low-relief jug

Brushes: medium; fine

Palette: acid yellow; golden yellow; light
 green; medium green; dark green

Paint used: solvent-based ceramic paint

Paint alternatives: *water-based ceramic
 paints; acrylic paint

Polyurethane varnish or glaze: for solvent-
 based ceramic paint

* requires baking

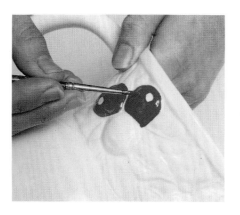

1 *Begin by painting some lemons acid yellow. Vary them, so that one group has 2 acid yellow lemons, the next group, 1, and so on. Leave a narrow white line around each lemon, and leave the seed cases and small circles at the base of the fruit white. Leave to dry.*

2 *Work your way around the relief pattern, painting the remaining fruit a rich, golden yellow. Using two yellows creates a sense of depth and variety. Again, leave a narrow white line around each fruit, and leave to dry.*

3 *Use light, medium and dark green for the leaves, for variety and interest. Start with the palest green, painting roughly a third of the leaves, evenly spaced apart, but don't worry about being too exact. Leave the central midrib of each leaf white, and a narrow white line around each leaf. Leave to dry.*

4 *Paint a third of the leaves medium green, again spacing them evenly. Paint the narrow base of the jug green and leave to dry, as before.*

5 *Paint the remaining leaves dark green and leave to dry. If using water-based ceramic paint, bake according to the instructions on page 144.*

6 *Now paint the rim (or the handle) in acid yellow leaving a narrow white line at the lower line. Once dry, varnish with polyurethane varnish or the glaze provided specially by the ceramic paint manufacturers for this purpose.*

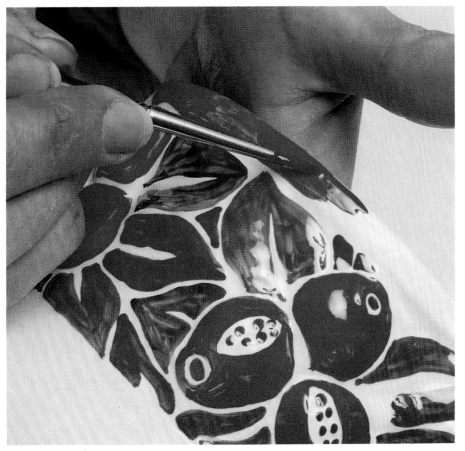

SPICE STORAGE JARS

These Provençal-style storage jars will brighten up any kitchen. Six different designs are shown, and you could try them all, or repeat the one you like best, changing the label wording as necessary, or invent your own patterns. Swatches of Provençal fabrics or wallpaper samples are obvious starting points.

The storage jars shown have four flat sides, each curved along the top edge. Flat-faced storage jars are widely available and easier to paint than round ones. If you can't find flat-sided jars with curved tops, you can draw a curve on tracing paper using a compass, then transfer it with carbon paper onto the jar. Storage jars come in larger sizes, for flour, sugar, rice and so on, and you can scale up these patterns to match the jar. Water-based ceramic paint is used here, but if you want to use vitrified enamels or solvent-based paint, adjust the technique accordingly (see pages 144–5).

The rich, bright colours and simple, small, repetitive motifs of these spice jars are based on Provençal cotton fabrics, which could be used for kitchen curtains, tablecloths or even table napkins. On a larger scale, Provençal-style wallpaper could be used to carry through the South of France theme, perhaps with toning paint on cupboards, or above a dado or picture rail. Big stoneware jars filled with branches of dried herbs would add a nice finishing touch.

Tools and materials

Flat-faced, white-glazed jars with stopper

Plain white paper

Pencils: hard; soft

Tracing paper

Masking tape

Masking paper

Scalpel or small scissors

Brushes: medium; fine

Carbon paper

Palette: light blue; red; yellow; green; dark blue

Paint used: *water-based ceramic paint

Paint alternative: solvent-based ceramic paint

Polyurethane varnish or glaze: for solvent-based ceramic paint

* requires baking

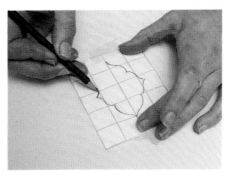

1 *Lay the jar flat onto a piece of white paper and, using a hard pencil, carefully draw round the edge of that face. (You may have to tuck your pencil in sideways to get the upper, curved edge.) This gives you the area available for decorating. Trace the shape onto tracing paper.*

3 *Trace the shape onto the back of the masking paper and, using a scalpel or a pair of small scissors, cut out the shape. Remove the backing from the masking paper and stick the shape onto the jar, matching the 4 points to the 4 marks on the jar. Make sure the masking paper is stuck down flat.*

2 *Cut this shape out and fold it in half, and then in half in the opposite direction, giving 4 quarters. These fold lines are the guidelines for repeating your design. Draw out a quarter of the finished design in 1 quarter: the double curved diagonal line comprising 1 side of the diamond, and the flower, halved vertically. Fold the tracing paper in half, first 1 way and then the other, to trace the shape onto each quarter.*

On the back of the tracing paper, using a soft pencil, mark the 4 corners of the shape. Lay the tracing paper, right side up, onto the flat side of the storage jar, making sure the edges are aligned, then fix with small pieces of masking tape. Using a hard pencil, mark the 4 points of the shape onto the jar. Remove the tracing paper.

4 *Paint the light blue background first. Start by painting the straight side and bottom edges and top, curved edge of the flat area, then work inward, painting in one direction only, to achieve an even, flat, dense coat. Leave to dry, then carefully peel the masking paper off using the edge of the scalpel blade to lift it. If any paint has bled under the masking paper, use a small brush dipped in water to remove it. Leave to dry thoroughly, then bake, according to instructions on page 144.*

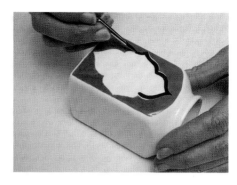

5 Paint a small band of red around the edge of the white shape, using a medium-sized brush. The natural variation of freehand painting is part of the charm, so do not worry about painting over the blue here and there.

6 Paint 2, small yellow flowers in the top and bottom of the diamond, vertically aligned, as shown. A gentle dab of the brush is all that is needed to make a petal. Make sure the flowers do not extend into the area reserved for the writing; imagine and draw a horizontal line connecting each pair of inward-facing points, and keep the flowers above and below them, respectively. Allow to dry, then bake.

7 Draw an outline on the tracing paper pattern to represent the red band, then write the name of the herb in large, simple letters in the central space. You can copy those shown, or use your own lettering. If you do your own try out several styles and avoid sophisticated or meticulous typefaces, which go against the spirit of the Provencal style.

Cut a piece of carbon paper the same size as the tracing paper. Stick this onto the jar, carbon-side down, using small pieces of masking tape. Lay the tracing over this, making sure the edges align with the edges of the jar. Using a hard pencil and pressing firmly, transfer the lettering onto the jar by writing over it again. Remove the carbon paper and tracing paper.

8 Using a fine paintbrush, paint dark blue dots randomly over the light blue. Using dark blue paint and a fine paintbrush, paint the lettering and a fine line around the flowers and both edges of the red band. Again, if the lines vary slightly in thickness and position, wavering a little over the blue and white, all the better!

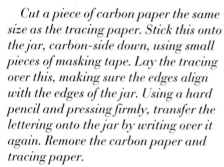

9 Paint a green dot in the centre of each flower, and paint the lid green, brushing in one direction only to achieve a dense, even coat. You may have to paint 2 coats, allowing the first coat to dry before applying the second. Allow to dry, then bake.

ORIENTAL BOWL

Blue and white ceramics are a centuries-old tradition, with the classic Oriental willow garden pattern and its many variations being the most famous. However, blue and white Persian tiles and ceramics, and nineteenth-century American blue and white spongeware, are equally attractive. Whatever the provenance of the motif, blue and white always look crisp and clean. You could, of course, interpret the design here in other colourways: perhaps rich russets and reds, or pastels or sunny yellows. Use the bowl to display fresh flowerheads or pot-pourri.

Freehand drawing is called for, but you can practise the swirly scrolls on paper until you are confident. When drawing on the ceramic, you can rub out the marker pen lines as often as you like, with a damp cloth, until you are satisfied. A scratching technique is also used, to create the sharp, white linear highlights to the motifs, but you could leave thin white lines around the motifs, when you paint the medium-blue infill, instead.

This blue and white, hand-painted ceramic bowl, filled with a branch of camellia in bud, has Oriental overtones. For authenticity, place a heavy metal, ikebana-style flower pinholder, available from Oriental shops, in the bottom of the bowl, to support the flower stem. Alternatively, you could simply float open camellia blossoms in the water-filled bowl.

Tools and materials

White-glazed bowl

Marker pen

Tape measure

Brushes: medium; fine

Scalpel

Damp cloth

Palette: light blue; medium blue; dark blue

Paint used: solvent-based ceramic paint

Paint alternative: *water-based ceramic
    paint

Polyurethane varnish or glaze: for solvent-
    based ceramic paint

* requires baking

1 *Mark out a horizontal line following the rim line of the bowl. To measure a line, use a cloth tape measure to mark points 6cm/2³⁄sin down from the rim all the way round. Join these up with a marker pen in a smooth line.*

    Draw the decorative scrolls onto the bowl with a black marker pen, above that line. Combine horizontal, undulating lines with graceful, curling 'C' shapes, singly or doubly, arching away from or toward each other, for the basic motif; no two adjacent scrolls face in the same direction. To create an overall pattern, draw parts of motifs, cut off by the rim and base, as if the pattern extended indefinitely.

2 *Using a medium-sized brush, paint the scrolls light blue. Try to keep the tone evenly flat and dense. Allow to dry.*

3 *Paint medium blue over all the remaining area above the horizontal line. Paint up to the edges of the scrolls first, then fill in the remaining white areas. Leave to dry.*

4 *Using a scalpel blade, scratch around the edges of the light blue scrolls to reveal the white beneath. This technique gives an uneven, broken edge; use a damp cloth to wipe away the paint chips.*

5 *Using a fine paintbrush, paint a dark blue line around each scroll, to add depth and contrast to the pattern. Leave visible as much of the white as possible. Leave to dry.*

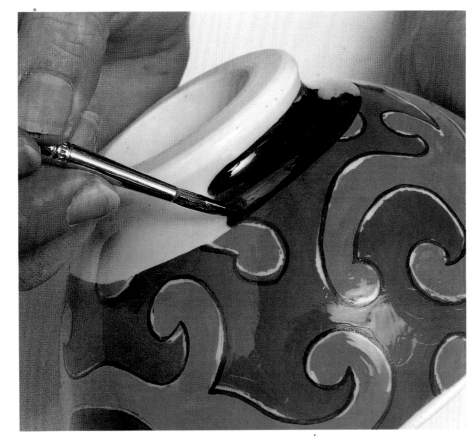

6 *Using the same dark blue and a larger brush, paint the base as far as its natural rim, which is left white. Aim for a flat, solid tone. Leave to dry. When dry, varnish or glaze for extra durability.*

BATHROOM TILES AND BORDER

These stencilled, hand-painted and sponged fish look well in the watery setting of a bathroom. Stylized, simplified and painted black, the options for variation lie in the angling of the fish and their positioning on the wall. You can arrange them in diagonal, horizontal or vertical stripes or alternating chequerboards, or as a single ring or border of fish around the splashback or shower area. You could also alternate another design such as sea shells, starfish, boats or even mermaids with the fish, or use just a single motif but with alternate

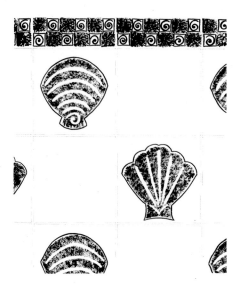

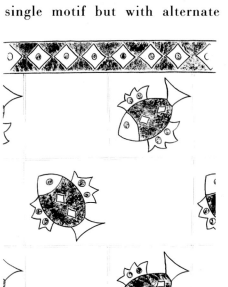

colours. Dark rich blue is as effective as black, and a bit more nautical.

You can buy plain border tiles or make your own by cutting a tile in half with a tile cutter, but buy more tiles than you need, to allow for mistakes. Most bathroom tiles are 15cm/ 6in square, and the measurements are based on this, but if your tiles differ, simply adjust the measurements. You can also decorate *in situ* tiles with solvent-based cold ceramic paint; the painted tiles will need a few coats of varnish to ensure waterproofing (see page 141 for more details).

These black and white painted tiles are designed to provide a theatrical backdrop for a collection of black and white ceramics, green glass and delicate sea ferns. The simple, black and white sponged stencil fish pattern is deliberately restrained in tone, so you can add splashes of bright colours and change them as often as you wish, without risk of colours clashing.

Tools and materials

White-glazed, border wall tiles: sufficient to
 cover border area (or tiles cut in half)

White-glazed wall tiles, 15cm/6in square:
 sufficient to cover area

Plain white paper: 2 sheets

Pencils: hard; soft

Metal ruler

Tracing paper

Carbon paper: 2 sheets

Scissors

Masking tape

Cutting board

Masking paper

Marker pen

Scalpel

Sponge or tissue

Palette: black

Paint used: *water-based ceramic paint

Paint alternatives: solvent-based ceramic
 paint; acrylic; quick-drying stencil paint

Polyurethane varnish or glaze

* requires baking

Main tiles

Border tiles

1 *Draw out a 15 × 15cm/6 × 6in
square and a 15 × 7.5cm/6 × 3in
rectangle on plain white paper, to
represent the tile and border tile,
respectively. On these two shapes, draw
out your motifs. Lay pieces of tracing
paper over the designs and trace.*

 *Cut 2 pieces of carbon paper,
roughly the same size as the tile and
border tile. Place them face down onto
the tiles, using small pieces of masking
tape to keep them in position, then
place the relevant pattern tracing on
top and stick it down. Using a hard
pencil, trace the motifs onto the tiles.*

2 *Take the same tracings, turn them
over (for a mirror image) and lay each
one over the backing side of two pieces
of masking paper. Hold them in
position on a cutting board with
masking tape and trace off the design
onto the back of the masking paper
with a marker pen. Lift off.*

3 *Keeping the masking paper,
backing-side up, on a cutting board,
held firmly in place with masking tape,
use a scalpel to cut out the areas to be
sponged: the body of the fish, the eye,
and four fin dots. Keep the 2 small
diamonds for the centre of the fish. For
the border tiles, cut out the diamond
shapes, and the central dots.*

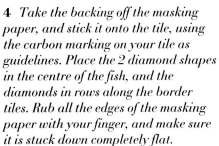

4 Take the backing off the masking paper, and stick it onto the tile, using the carbon marking on your tile as guidelines. Place the 2 diamond shapes in the centre of the fish, and the diamonds in rows along the border tiles. Rub all the edges of the masking paper with your finger, and make sure it is stuck down completely flat.

5 Have your paint ready in a small, shallow pot. Take a small piece of sponge or scrumpled-up tissue, dab it in the paint and dab off the excess paint onto an old tile or scrap paper until you're happy with the density of coverage. Dab it onto the tiles, in the cut-out areas. Do not be afraid to go over the edges of the masking paper.

6 Once the stencil is completely filled in, leave to dry, then lift off the masking paper, using the end of a scalpel to lever up the paper.

Using a medium-sized paintbrush, paint the outline around the fish motif and diamond border. Don't worry about immaculately even strokes; the charm is in its freehand style.

Bake if using water-based ceramic paint, and varnish. If the tiles are being painted in situ, coat with polyurethane varnish or glaze.

SOAP DISH

These watery creatures add a lively visual touch to a bathroom, whether painted neutral black and white as in the fish motif scheme shown on page 84, or more colourfully as here. The green and yellow used here is inspired by green and yellow glycerine soaps, their translucence adding to the aquatic imagery. Alternatively, use turquoise or ultramarine blue instead of yellow, or the colourways of bathroom towels, walls or floor. For a co-ordinated effect, decorate other ceramic bathroom items, such as framed mirrors or tissue box covers,

with a similar motif. (You might include a few black tadpoles, for a naturalistic touch!) For a kitchen soap dish, you could substitute a chicken, sheep or cow motif, against a grassy green background, or a vegetable or fruit motif.

Hard-wearing water-based ceramic paint is a sensible choice for this project, since it can stand up to heavy use and moisture. A flat-based soap dish is easier to decorate than one with a round base – a point worth keeping in mind when buying the ceramic for painting.

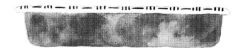

Inspired by the colours of bright glycerine soap, this soap dish, with its green, yellow, black and white aquatic theme, adds a fresh and humorous note to a bathroom. The colour-washed terracotta pots can be used indoors as well as in the garden, continuing the theme of other hand-painted ceramic objects, as here, or picking up colours from the walls, carpets or furnishings.

Tools and materials

Small oblong, white-glazed dish with sides

Brushes: fine; medium

Pencils: soft; hard

Plain white paper

Tracing paper

Carbon paper

Masking tape

Palette: green; yellow; black

Paint used: *water-based ceramic paint

* requires baking

1 *Paint the base yellow. Using a fine brush, paint round the inside edge of the base, then use a larger brush to infill the middle. Spread the paint thinly, for a colour-washed effect, but do not dilute the water-based ceramic paint, since dilution affects its durability. Allow to dry, then bake, according to the instructions on page 144.*

2 *Draw a stylized frog on plain paper, keeping in mind the size of the base. (It may help to trace the base onto another piece of tracing paper, place it over the frog and trace the frog, then trace it in twice more, to make sure the size is suitable.) Trace it onto tracing paper. Cut a piece of carbon paper roughly the same size, then stick it, carbon-side out, on the underside of the tracing paper. Hold the tracing paper slightly above the inside of the dish, and move it around to get the best position. Stick it on the ceramic base, using masking tape to hold it firm. Using a hard pencil, draw round the frog to transfer the image onto the base. Do this twice more, to form a rough triangle of frogs.*

3 *Using a fine brush, paint the frogs black from the outline in, spreading the paint thinly to achieve a watery effect. Allow to dry, then bake.*

4 *Paint the inner sides of the dish bright green. Start from the yellow edge, working the strokes along and up, and stopping where the sides curve to form the rim. Tackle an area about 5cm/2in square at a time; it becomes easier as you proceed. Leave to dry.*

Using a medium-sized brush, paint green dots randomly over the yellow base.

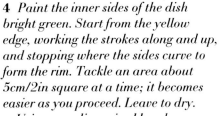

5 *Paint the outer sides of the dish green. Paint carefully along the edge under the top rim, working the strokes along and down, tackling a small area at a time. Stop at the bottom edge or continue slightly under the rim. Leave to dry, then bake.*

6 *Using a fine brush, paint a black outline around the frogs, leaving small gaps of yellow here and there. If you want, paint circles with central black dots for frog spawn effect. Leave to dry.*

7 *Using a soft pencil, mark in a stripe motif at the 4 corners of the rim, then complete the rim pattern one section at a time, spacing out groups of 3 vertical and 4 horizontal strokes so they alternate. Using a fine brush and black paint, paint the motif. Allow to dry, then bake.*

FRUIT BOWL

This is a freehand project, and the loosely drawn oranges, leaves and flowers do not demand sophisticated artistic skill. The black outlines help define the shapes; straight lines down the centres of the leaves, for example, represent midribs, and circles represent flower centres. You could substitute apples, pears, pineapples or lemons for the oranges, or a mixture of fruit, adjusting the background colour accordingly.

Neither solvent-based nor water-based ceramic paints should come in contact with the mouth or food, so paint only the outside of the bowl. If you intend to fill it with overhanging grapes and so on, leave an unpainted and unvarnished rim around the top. Solvent-based ceramic paint is used here, but if you use water-based paint, remember to bake the bowl after each colour is applied, according to the instructions on page 144.

The rich burgundy shown gives this bowl autumnal overtones, and also adds to the Forties look of the stylized fruit. If the background were painted blue you would create a sunny, Mediterranean feel; Chinese yellow, on the other hand, perhaps with pinky-red strawberries, would take it firmly into the Sixties. The background could also be left white, with a fruit border or central band painted around the bowl. Fabrics of the Forties often featured stylized fruit, and would be a good starting point.

Tools and materials

Large round, white-glazed bowl

Marker pen

Brushes: medium; fine

Palette: rich burgundy; lime green; dark
  green; black; orange-yellow; lilac

Paint used: solvent-based ceramic paint

Paint alternative: *water-based ceramic
  paint

Polyurethane varnish or glaze: for solvent-
  based ceramic paint

* requires baking

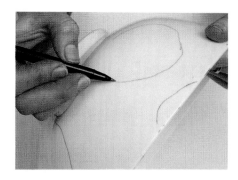

1 *Using a black marker pen, draw 4 or 5 roughly circular, whole oranges onto the bowl, leaving space between them for leaves and flowers. Draw 4 or 5 cut-off oranges along the top rim and base, as if the design extended indefinitely.*

2 *Using a medium-sized brush, paint the oranges, spreading the paint thinly to give a water-washed tone. Leave to dry.*

3 *Draw stylized flowers peeping out from behind the oranges. Draw one flower behind every whole orange, with a cut-off circle representing the centre.*

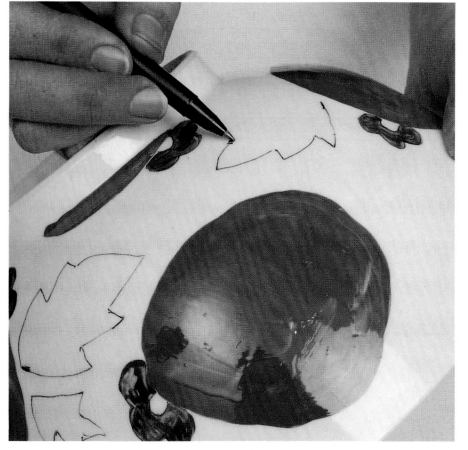

4 *Paint the flowers lilac, using a small brush and spreading the paint thinly. Leave the centres white.*

5 *Using a black marker pen, draw the leaves, one large and one small, for each orange. Space them to fill the background area evenly, so there are*

no big gaps. Again, draw part or half leaves attached to oranges along the rim and base of the bowl, to balance the design.

6 *Paint all the small leaves lime green, spreading the paint thinly. Leave to dry.*

7 *Using the same method, paint the large leaves dark green and leave to dry.*

8 *Paint the ground rich burgundy. Starting with a small brush, paint round the fruit shapes, leaving a narrow white outline. Use a larger brush for infill. Spread the paint thinly, so the brushstrokes remain visible, for textural variety. Paint the rim and base carefully, for a tidy finish.*

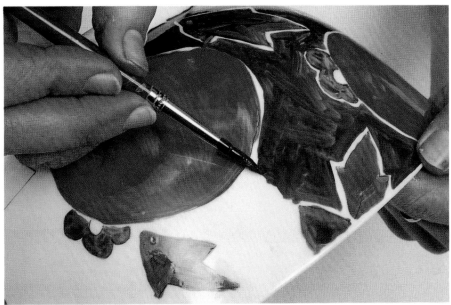

9 *Using a medium-sized brush and black paint, paint loosely around the images. Vary the pressure on the brush, so the line is sometimes thick, other times thin. Paint the midribs in the leaves and the circular centres in the flowers.*

10 *Using dark green, paint the rim at the base. Spread the paint thinly, so the brushmarks show and emphasize the hand-painted quality of the design. Coat the paint with varnish or glaze when dry.*

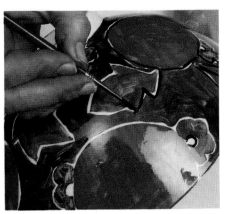

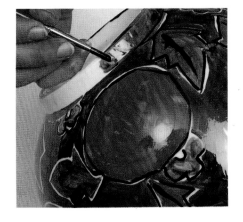

COUNTRY QUILT VASE

Patience, more than skill, is needed to create this pretty flower vase, based on the rich colours and simple motifs of American patchwork quilts. It is also a design that can be easily simplified. You could, for example, paint the medium blue stripes around the sides, decorate them with leaves and dots, or even tiny dots and random brushmarks, and leave it at that. Alternatively, you could paint the checked band around the rim and centre, as shown, and decorate the remaining white area with blue leaves.

Solvent-based ceramic paint is used, although less durable than water-based paint. The vase may be used for fresh flowers as long as you treat the outside with care when rinsing it. The vase is also ideal for a country-inspired display of dried flowers, foliage and seed pods: dried artemisia, bulrushes, honesty, wheat, hops, corn and barley, with massed red cockscomb or amaranthus.

The shape of the vase is simple, timeless and attractive in its own right, but if you are new to ceramic painting, you might find it easier to use a straight-sided, cylindrical vase.

This American country vase uses traditional Pennyslvania Dutch-style colours of red, caramel, blue and white, to create a period feel. The design however is quite contemporary, updating old-fashioned motifs by incorporating and juxtaposing them in broad modern bands.

Tools and materials

Urn-shaped, white-glazed jar with neck and
    lip

Tape measure

Marker pen

Brushes: large; fine

Palette: light blue; yellow ochre; dark blue;
    red; dark red

Paint used: solvent-based ceramic paint

Paint alternative: *water-based ceramic
    paint

Polyurethane varnish or glaze: for solvent-
    based ceramic paint

* requires baking

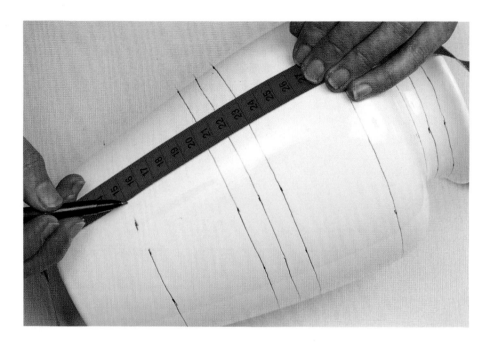

1 *Measure from the rim to the neck
base and, using a marker pen, mark it
with a dot. Continue measuring around
the vase, then join the dots to form a
line. Using a flexible tape measure,
measure from the line to the vase base,
laying the tape flat along the contours.
Halve this dimension, then mark the
half-way point all the way around and*
*join the dots. Measure and mark 2
horizontal lines 1.25cm/½in above and
below the central line, for the white
band. Measure, mark and draw a line
half-way between the top edge of the
band and the base line of the neck, and
another, half-way between the bottom
edge of the strip and the vase base.*

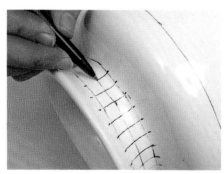

2 *Measure from the vase rim to the
neck base line, and divide it into thirds.
Measure, mark and draw 2 horizontal
lines, ⅓ and ⅔ of the way down, to
form the horizontal band of the check.
Measure the rim circumference and
divide it by the width of the central
band. You need an even number of
spaces for the check to work, so adjust
the width of the spaces as necessary.*

3 *Mark the spaces all the way around
the outer rim and neck base aligning
the dots; then join vertically to create
the check.*

4 *Using a small brush along the boundaries and a larger brush for infill, paint the light blue stripes. Aim for a flat, evenly dense tone; you may have to let the first coat dry and then apply a second coat. Leave to dry.*

5 *Using the same technique, paint the yellow ochre bands. If you leave a narrow white stripe between the colours it adds a sharp crispness, but you can omit this detail. Leave to dry.*

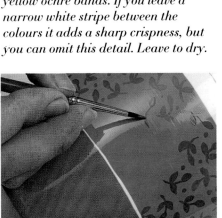

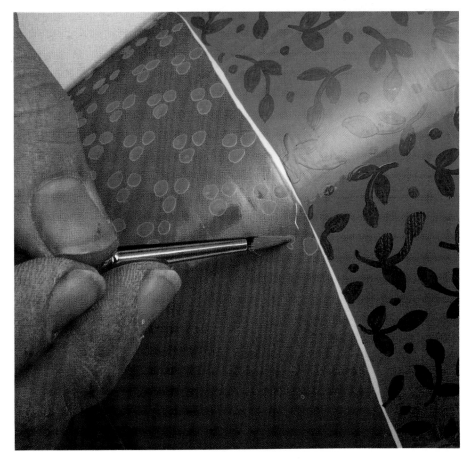

6 *Using a small brush and dark blue paint, paint the 3-leaf motif, freehand, on both blue stripes. Paint the curved stems first, angled randomly, then add the leaves and the tiny dots. (For a simpler version, paint single leaves, or just the dots.)*

7 *Using a small brush and medium blue paint, paint the 3-dot, triangle motif on the ochre bands. Start from the top edge down, working in horizontal rows, doing a small section at a time. Stagger the triangles in the second row to create the diagonal effect shown, but make alternate rows align vertically. Leave to dry.*

8 *Using a marker pen, draw squares, fairly evenly spaced, in the centre of the middle white band and on the neck band.*

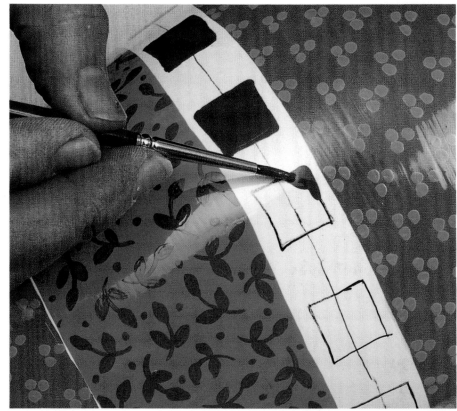

9 *Using a small brush and red paint, paint these squares and leave to dry. Do not worry if the paint is slightly uneven or the edges are rough.*

10 *Using a small brush and red paint, carefully paint the central horizontal stripe around the neck. Leave to dry.*

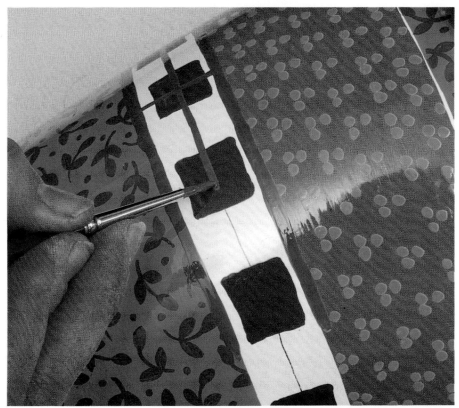

11 *Using a small brush, paint a thin, dark blue stripe around the top and bottom edge of the central white band. Leave to dry, then paint a thinner, parallel stripe through the centre, overpainting the red squares. Leave to dry.*

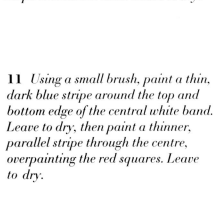

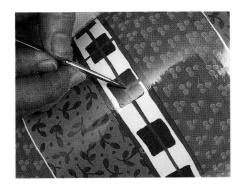

12 *Using a small brush, paint vertical dark blue lines through the centre of each red square, as shown.*

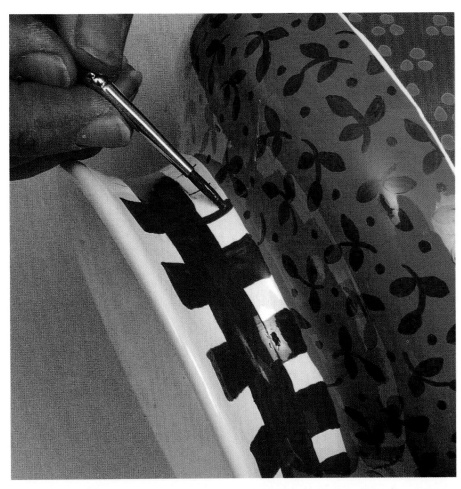

13 *Using a small brush, paint the vertical stripes of the checked pattern on the neck, using the lines drawn in Steps 1 and 8 as a guide. Leave to dry.*

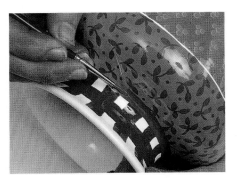

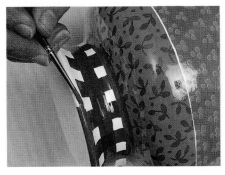

14 *Using a small brush, paint freehand a dark blue line about 6mm/¼in wide between the red check and blue-patterned band. (If you feel you need to measure it, mark and re-draw the bottom edge of the band as in Step 1.) Allow to dry.*

15 *Paint a similar, narrow, dark blue band around the top edge of the vase.*

16 *Using a small brush and dark red paint, overpaint the central squares of each check, where horizontals and verticals overlap. Leave to dry, then coat with varnish or glaze for extra durability.*

TERRACOTTA POTS

This lively-looking group of freehand painted terracotta pots gives added style to a conservatory, garden room or sheltered patio. The pots would also suit a plant-filled living room or kitchen, or even a large hall landing with a sunny windowsill.

To paint terracotta, you can use matt emulsion or solvent-based cold ceramic paints; with an undercoat to seal the porous surface, or without an undercoat as shown here. This last method creates an uneven finish, which works well with the rough nature of terracotta. If you're doing several pots, it is worth trying out the different options, to discover which you prefer; solvent-based paint will weather and fade if the pots are placed outdoors, but that adds to their charm. However, note that some terracotta pots are not frost-hardy.

Inexpensive, traditionally shaped pots are shown, but other options include round, Ali Baba pots, perhaps decorated with a series of parallel, horizontal zigzags. More expensive,

Italian terracotta urns with bas-relief motifs, such as swags, cherubs, leaves and flowers, could have the motifs picked out in subtle neutral or stone colours to give the appearance of being carved out of natural stone. Some garden centres have old, hand-thrown terracotta flowerpots, which have a lovely grainy texture and slight asymmetry, though usually rather narrow rims. You can achieve a similar effect by leaving brand-new terracotta pots outside for a few months, to expose them to the elements. If you age the pots before painting, remember to scrub them clean and dry thoroughly before painting, since algae and salts can build up on the surface and prevent paint adhering.

A colour scheme can be based on a decor or to complement the plants grown, ideally both! In this case, the sunny yellow and fresh green of spring daffodils served as the inspiration, but yellow pansies, polyanthus or wallflowers could also fill the pots in spring; followed by yellow French or African marigolds, dwarf dahlias, nasturtiums, black-eyed Susans or bright yellow coleus in summer; and bright yellow pot chrysanthemums in autumn or winter.

Tools and materials

Terracotta pots with deep rim:
    circumference 52.5cm/21in
Ribbon: 70cm/28in
Pencil: soft
Tape measure
Brushes: medium; large
Turpentine or clear rubbing alcohol
Palette: green; lime green; yellow
Paint used: solvent-based ceramic paint
Paint alternatives: matt emulsion or
    undercoat; * water-based ceramic paint

* requires baking

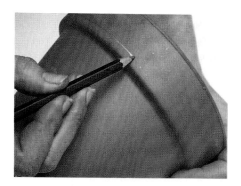

1 *Using a soft pencil, draw 2 parallel, horizontal lines around the top and bottom of the rim. Many terracotta pots have natural ridges here, but if not, use a cloth tape to measure 1.25cm/¹/₂in down from the top and up from the bottom, marking at regular intervals with a soft pencil, then joining all the points together.*

2 *Using a cloth tape measure, measure around the top of the pot to work out the border pattern. The pot shown measures 52.5cm/21in around the top; this is divided into 7.5cm/3in intervals, giving 7 zigzags, evenly spaced apart. Work out the spacings and number of zigzags to suit your pot; you can have 5 or 9 intervals.*

3 *Using the interval marks as guidelines for the zigzags – 1 zigzag fits between every 2 marks – draw a double* *horizontal row of zigzags, as shown, keeping the lines uneven for a more naturalistic, or primitive, effect.*

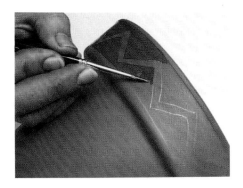

4 *Paint the green triangles, leaving the zigzags and top and bottom rims terracotta, as shown. If you are using solvent-based paints, dip your brush into turpentine occasionally, to thin the paint and give an uneven, hand-painted tone. With emulsion or water-based ceramic paint, dip the brush occasionally in water, to achieve the same effect. Do not dilute more than 20 per cent or the viscosity is affected. Leave to dry.*

5 *Using the horizontal zigzags as a guide, roughly crossing the base point of the alternate zigzags, draw a vertical zigzag onto the pot, working your way around the rim. Make the width of each zigzag about 1.25cm/½in. Don't try to make them identical; freehand variation adds interest.*

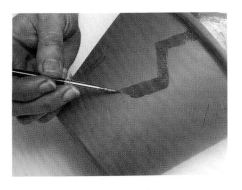

6 *When all the zigzags are drawn, paint them lime green. For a more vibrant, opaque effect, you can paint 2 coats, but let the first coat dry thoroughly before applying the second.*

7 *Using a large brush, randomly dot the area between the zigzags with yellow paint, and leave to dry. If using water-based paint, for extra durability and water-resistance, bake according to the instructions on page 144.*

CHILDREN'S BOWL

Place this decorative set, painted with solvent-based ceramic paint, on a shelf in a nursery or playroom. Simple, easily identifiable motifs go down best with children, and though a stylized train engine inspired by old-fashioned wooden toys is shown here, a car, rocking horse, teddy bear, doll or other childhood image would do equally well. If you are unsure of a motif, look for inspiration in children's colouring or reading books, or even greeting cards designed for children. You could do a series of decorative bowls, each one with a different image based on the child's own toys, but linked by the use of common colours.

This design has a Victorian colour scheme of rich ochre, Prussian blue and red, but you could use bright yellow, pink and bright green, or primary red, blue and yellow, for a more contemporary effect. The dots add a lively touch and, being fairly random, are easy for even a beginner to achieve.

The bowl shown has a wide, flat bottom, which is much easier for drawing and painting on than rounded bowls – a point to be kept in mind when buying the ceramics.

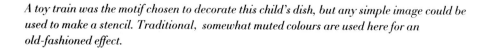

A toy train was the motif chosen to decorate this child's dish, but any simple image could be used to make a stencil. Traditional, somewhat muted colours are used here for an old-fashioned effect.

Tools and materials

White-glazed, flat bowl

Ruler or tape measure

Compass

Scissors

Masking paper

Pencil: hard

Brushes: fine; medium; large

Scalpel

Turpentine or clear rubbing alcohol

Tracing paper

Carbon paper

Masking tape

Palette: Prussian blue; yellow ochre; red; white; black

Paint used: solvent-based ceramic paint

Paint alternative: *water-based ceramic paint

Polyurethane varnish or glaze: for solvent-based ceramic paint

* requires baking

1 *Using a ruler or tape measure, measure the diameter of the base. Use a compass to draw a circle with the same diameter on a piece of masking paper. Cut the circle out, take the backing off, and stick the masking paper onto the base of the bowl. Rub the edges of the paper with a cloth or your finger, to make sure it is flat and evenly adhered, with no bubbles.*

2 *Paint the inside rim of the bowl dark blue. The masking paper defines the lower edge, and the natural rim of the bowl defines the outer edge. (As an alternative, you could paint from the masking paper outward, over the edge of the rim and down the outside, to the base.) Try to apply a flat, even, dense coat. Leave to dry thoroughly, then lift off the masking paper, using a scalpel blade to gently lever it up. If any paint has bled underneath, take it off with a fine paintbrush dipped in turpentine.*

3 *Draw the train onto tracing paper. Cut a piece of carbon paper the same size and lay it face down onto the centre of the bowl, using masking tape to keep it in place. Lay and stick the tracing on top, making sure that the image is central. Trace the image with a hard pencil, then lift off the tracing paper and carbon paper.*

4 *Paint the body of the train yellow ochre, painting around the edges first and then infilling the middle. Try to get a flat, even density. Leave to dry.*

Paint the centre of the train, the window frame and the button top of the engine in blue. Leave to dry.

5 & 6 *Paint the funnel and wheels red, then, using the same colour, paint the outside of the bowl following the natural edges moulded into the bowl. Leave to dry.*

7 & 8 *Using a medium-sized paintbrush, paint white dots randomly over the red outer surface of the bowl, then paint the dark blue rim and stripe in the centre of the train. Leave to dry.*

9 *Paint the centre of the train wheels black. Finally, outline the train with a fine black line, as shown, but if you aren't confident about your freehand brushstrokes, omit this outline. When dry, cover the paint with varnish or glaze.*

MOSAIC MIRROR FRAME

This project is great fun to do, but it does require patience. Fitting the mosaic pieces together is rather like doing a jigsaw puzzle. Once the technique is mastered, however, the possibilities are endless.

Start with simple patterns and a two-colour design before you progress to more complicated variations. For instance, you could simply mark diagonals in each corner of a frame, and make the vertical sections one colour, and the horizontal sections another. Grouting can provide a third colour, if you like.

Although a mirror frame is shown here, you can use the same technique for smaller photograph frames, perhaps doing several for a group display of family photographs on a mantelpiece or occasional table. Or you could cover a box or small table top with mosaic and try using pieces of patterned or textured tiles for an even richer effect.

The project shown is 50 × 70cm/ 20 × 28in; you can make a larger or smaller one, but the larger it is, the heavier. You can leave the edge as it is, or trim it with thin batons or rods (available from D.I.Y. shops) tacked into the sides of the wood base. Paint the baton edging blue, to match, or a metallic colour. Mirror glass can be bought cut to size or you can buy a standard mirror, new or second-hand, and work your dimensions around it. Glue mirrors with strong P.V.A. adhesive onto the wood.

Chemicals in grouting react with some ceramic paints, lifting them off the surface, so you need to test the paint first with the grout you intend to use. If the grout does rub the paint off, coat it first with polyurethane varnish for protection.

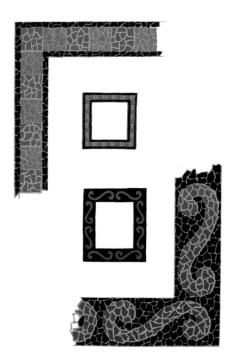

This mirror frame is based on an Italian mosaic theme, and features a rich combination of blue scrollwork motifs against a black ground. It is made by colouring and then breaking ceramic tiles, which are then stuck on to a frame in a mosaic pattern.

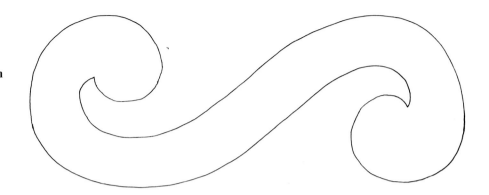

Tools and materials

16 white-glazed wall tiles

Plywood: 50 × 70 × 9cm/20 × 28 × 3½in

White glue (P.V.A. adhesive)

Large brush

Tea or dish towel

Freezer bags

Hammer

Large sheet of newspaper

Pencils: hard; soft

Tape measure

Tracing paper

Masking tape

Carbon paper

Thick marker pen

Tile-on-wood glue and spatula

Sponge

Grouting (from decorators' suppliers)

Soft cloth

Palette: blue; black

Paint used: *water-based ceramic paint

**Paint alternative: car spray paint (test on
    grouting first)**

* requires baking

1 *Buy a piece of plywood 50 × 70 ×
9cm/20 × 28 × 3½in. Using a large
brush, coat it all over with P.V.A. glue
and leave to dry for 24 hours. This seals
the wood and helps the tile glue to stick.*

2 *Paint 6 tiles blue and 10 black. (It is
better to have too many than too few.)
Leave to dry and then bake according
to the instructions on page 144. When
dry, place 2 tiles, the same colour, face
down on a tea or dish towel and fold
over the edges. This protects you and
prevents the pieces scattering when
smashed.*

3 *Using a hammer, smash the tiles
repeatedly, checking from time to time
until they are roughly broken into
manageable fragments. Keep the blue
and black pieces in separate bags.
Continue until all the tiles are smashed
or, if working over several days, smash
the tiles as needed.*

4 Draw a 50 × 70cm/20 × 28in rectangle on newsprint. Draw an inner rectangle, 39 × 60cm/16 × 24in. Draw a scroll within each section, to get 4 pairs of opposite-facing scrolls. You can draw 1 scroll shape on carbon paper and trace it off on each block, flipping over left to right and top to bottom to get mirror images.

Trace the frame, guidelines and scrolls onto a large sheet of tracing paper. Tape carbon paper carbon-side down on one corner of the wood. (Or you can cover the frame area with several sheets.) Tape the tracing onto the wood, matching the corners. Using a sharp pencil, trace all the scrolls, lifting, moving and re-taping the carbon paper as necessary. Remove the paper and go over the scrolls with a thick marker pen.

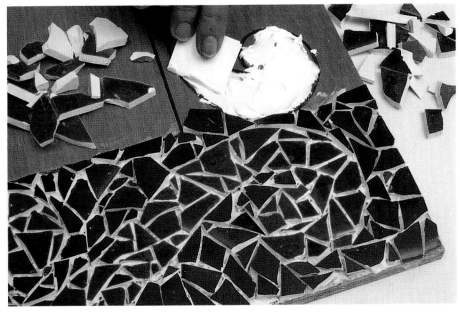

6 Allow 24 hours for the glue to dry, then grout. Dip a small piece of household sponge into a tub of grout, then spread over the mosaic with a circular motion. Continue until the grout fills all the gaps and is level with the mosaics. Allow to dry for 1 hour, then polish with a soft cloth, rubbing off the excess grout. If any paint should lift during this process, just touch it up when you have finished.

5 Starting with blue, work on a few centimetres/inches at a time. Using the nozzle, squirt tile glue onto a small section of 1 scroll. Spread the glue 3mm/⅛in thick over the area within the scroll, using a small spatula, and removing any excess.

Working from the top edge of the scroll down, press 1 mosaic piece at a time onto the glue. Keep the spaces between them evenly narrow, for grouting. If you make a mistake, lift the mosaic immediately, rub off the glue and start again. Wipe off any glue on the tiles as you go. Lay your hands over the newly done area, pressing stubborn ones down flat. Spread glue over an adjacent black area, pushing it up to the blue. Working from the scroll edge out, fill in the black tiles and repeat until the frame is covered. Always scrape off excess glue on the wood if you temporarily stop work, or the final surface will be uneven.

PAISLEY TEAPOT

The familiar, teardrop-shaped motif, curved at one end, goes back 2,500 years to ancient Babylon. Based on the shape of an unfurling date palm frond, it symbolized fertility and the Tree of Life, for palms provided not only food but also building materials, and thus, shelter. Today, paisley is a classic decorative motif on men's ties, shirts, women's scarves and upholstery fabrics.

This project is inspired by rich paisley shawls and spicy Indian colours. You could change the mood by substituting shades of green and yellow ochre, or creams and greys overlaid with black. If you find the pattern too busy, just paint the teapot red and then sponge it with orange, and detail with linear black paisley patterns.

If you are intending to use the teapot, use hard-wearing water-based ceramic paint and leave a broad rim unpainted and unglazed, baking after each colour is added; the same goes for cups, saucers, sugar bowls and milk jugs. If the pieces are only for decorative use, solvent-based paint is easier, and is used here.

The decoration of matching smaller objects, such as cups and saucers, jugs and sugar bowls, can be based on a single, simplified element taken from this teapot. Paint a bright base colour, then sponge over with another. If you feel confident and inspired, you can add an almost infinite amount of black-line detail, using a fine brush and a steady hand.

Tools and materials

White-glazed teapot

Tape measure

Marker pen

Tracing paper

Scissors

Pencils: hard; soft

Plain white paper

Tracing paper

Carbon paper

Masking tape

Brushes: medium; fine

Sponge or tissue

Old tile or scrap paper

Masking tape

Palette: dark red; yellow ochre; dark orange;
   bright orange; black

Paint used: solvent-based ceramic paint

Paint alternative: *water-based ceramic
   paint

Polyurethane varnish or glaze: for solvent-
   based ceramic paint

* requires baking

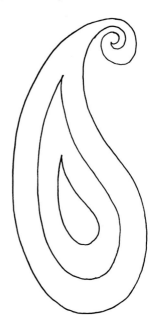

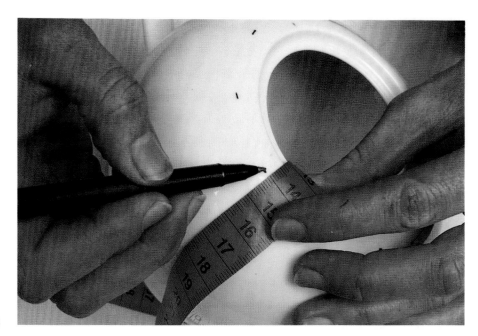

1 *Using a cloth tape measure and black marker pen, mark 8mm/¹⁄₃in down from the rim, all the way round* *the teapot, and join the dots together to form a band.*

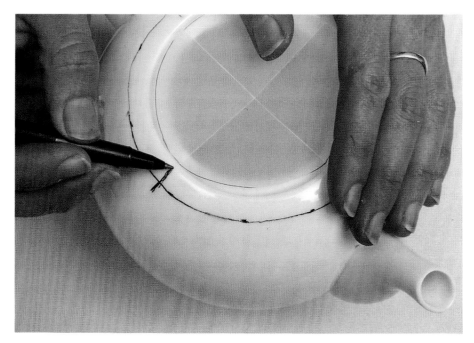

2 *Measure the diameter of the hole in the top. Draw a circle, the same size, onto tracing paper. Cut-out, fold in half, then quarters. Unfold, then rest flat in the hole, lining the folds up with the handle and spout. Mark the points where the folds touch the teapot, mid-* *way between the handle and spout. This divides the pot into halves, for setting out your design. Turn the pot upside down, and place the tracing paper circle on the base, lining up the folds as before, and mark the points onto the pot.*

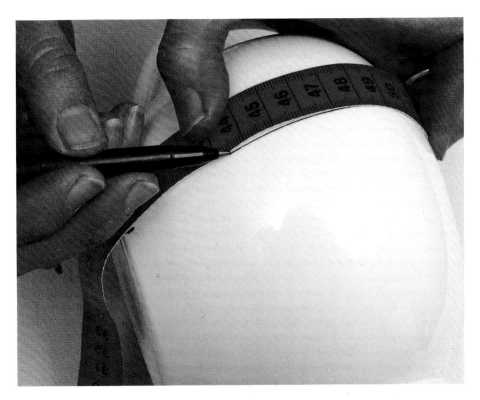

3 *Lay the tape measure over the body of the pot, along the contours and joining the upper and lower points. Draw a line along the tape measure edge. Repeat on the other side of the pot. This gives you your centre line.*

4 *Measure the height of the pot, and from the centre line to the spout, and along the circumference. Roughly draw a paisley shape on paper, slightly less than the pot's height, and half the measured width, at the shape's widest point. Trace it onto tracing paper, then cut it out 1cm/³/sin larger, all the way round. Lay it on the teapot, lining up the motif's outside edge with the centre line. Adjust or re-draw, if necessary, until it looks right. Cut a piece of carbon paper the same size.*

Stick together with masking tape, carbon-side down, then fix with masking tape in position on the pot. Using a hard pencil, draw over the lines on the tracing paper to transfer the motif to the pot. Remove the tracing and carbon paper. Separate them, turn over the tracing paper and stick it carbon-side down onto the carbon paper to reverse the image. Repeat as before, aligning the motif with its opposite, and trace onto the pot.

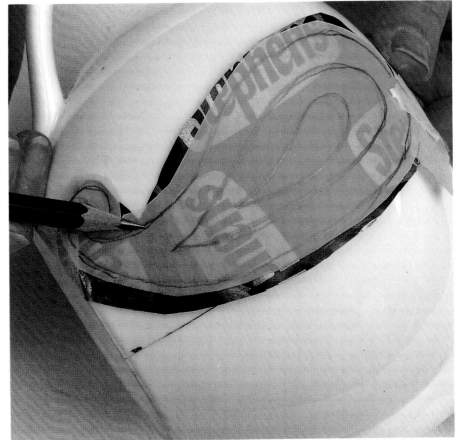

5 *Draw a diamond within a diamond between the motifs, as shown, and repeat on the other side. Trace or draw freehand a reverse curl next to each existing curl, one coming to a point at the handle base, the other at the spout base. Repeat, reversed, on the other side, to form a double curl.*

Draw a lozenge shape above the curls, either side of the handle and spout, as shown, and draw an inner lozenge. Draw 4, equal-sized scallops on each side of the pot. Start from the centre line and follow the curves of the motif, at least 1cm/³⁄₈in above them and 1cm/³⁄₈in below the line round the rim.

6 *Gently rub out the centre line, using a wet finger and taking care not to rub out the designs. Paint all the red areas, including the outside band of the motif, the diamond and oval shapes. The tone does not have to be even, as it is an underlayer. Leave to dry.*

7 *Paint the lid in red, but not the knob. Leave to dry. (If using water-based ceramic paint, bake the pot and lid according to the instructions on page 144.)*

8 *Paint the yellow ochre areas, including the scallops, paisley motifs, diamond and oval shapes. Paint up to the red, so no white shows; do not worry if you slightly go over the red. Paint the knob on the lid. Leave to dry. If using water-based paint, bake as before.*

9 *Paint all the remaining areas dark orange, but if you intend to use the pot, leave the area above the scallops white. Leave to dry, again baking if water-based paint is used.*

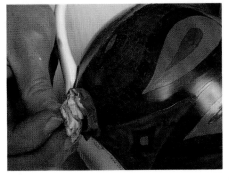

10 *Place bright orange paint in a shallow container. Dip a small piece of natural sponge or crumpled tissue into the paint, dab the excess onto scrap paper or white tile, then dab onto the pot. Repeat until the pot and lid, but not the knob, are textured. If you intend to use the pot, mask out the white area before sponging. Leave to dry, baking if water-based paint is used.*

11 *Using a small brush and black paint, outline the scallop, paisley, diamond and lozenge shapes. Outline the centres of the motifs. Decorate the paisley shapes with scallops and dots, as shown, or add more or less detail, as wished. Leave to dry or bake.*

12 *Decorate the lid with black paint; elongated dots are shown but, again, you can use your imagination. Leave to dry, bake the pot and lid, as before. If using solvent-based paint, coat the paint with varnish or glaze.*

HOLLY CHRISTMAS PLATTER

Stylized holly leaves and berries decorate the rim of this festive oval platter, and the gold outlines and gold-spattered centre add seasonal glamour. Although maroon and holly-berry red seem an unlikely combination, the maroon background adds a dense richness. You could leave the background white, or choose an equally rich ultramarine blue or even a stinging, Chinese yellow instead of maroon. You could also substitute silver, copper or bronze paint for the gold; an ultramarine blue background and silver detailing would be a wonderful combination.

Solvent-based ceramic paint is ideal for this display plate, especially as water-based paint does not come in metallic colours. You could, however, use the latter, omitting the gold in the design, and baking the plate after the addition of every colour. With experience, hand-painting the narrow, bright red rim band is easy, but if you are an absolute beginner, and worried about keeping an even thickness, you can omit that detail.

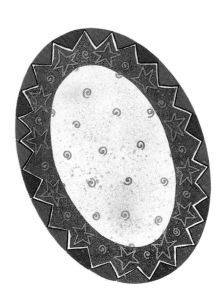

Display this festive painted plate heaped high with metallic Christmas tree balls, repeating the chosen colour theme, or a mixture of Christmas tree balls and pine cones, spray-painted in metallic colours or left natural. For a children's party, heap the plate with cellophane-wrapped candy canes, and metallic-paper-covered chocolate coins or Santa Clauses.

Tools and materials

White-glazed oval dish

Masking paper

Scissors

Scalpel

Pencils: hard; soft

Watercolour paper or flexible card

Fine marker pen

Brushes: medium; fine

Toothbrush or miniature spray gun

Turpentine or clear rubbing alcohol

Palette: maroon; bright red; gold; rich dark
  green

Paint used: solvent-based ceramic paint

Paint alternative: *water-based ceramic
  paint (though gold not in this range)

Polyurethane varnish or glaze: for solvent-
  based ceramic paint

* requires baking

1 *Cut out a rectangle of masking paper, roughly the size of the plate. Take the backing off and stick the paper onto the centre of the plate, pressing it flat from the centre outwards. Using a scalpel, cut around the inner, oval edge of the rim, to mask out the centre. Rub along the edge of the masking paper with your finger, then remove the excess.*

2 *Draw 2 or 3 stylized holly leaves, with an elongated oval for the central midrib, onto flexible card or watercolour paper. Don't use stencil paper here, as it is inflexible and will not shape itself to the curved rim. Give the leaves slightly different curving shapes to add interest to the design. Cut out the leaves and their centres, using a scalpel or small, sharp scissors.*

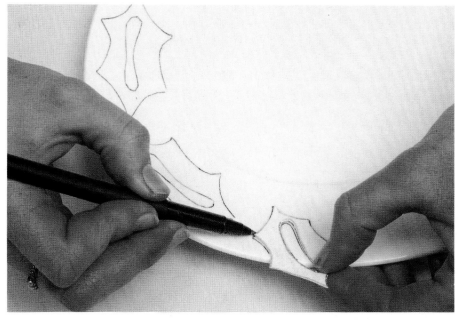

3 *Lay the leaf stencils, one at a time, onto the rim, and mark with a soft pencil where the first leaf starts. Check that the motif roughly fits, by placing and marking the stencils sequentially around the border leaving room for stems and a line top and bottom for the rim if wanted. (Half leaves are fine*

against the inner and outer rims, but try to avoid half leaves within the border itself.) If you have too much space between the first and last leaves, fill it with extra berries; if you have too little, angle the leaf. Aim for a natural, scattered effect. Next, trace the leaves in, using a fine marker pen or pencil.

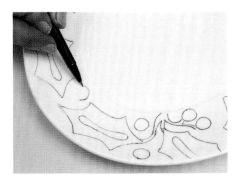

4 *Add the stems, some straight, others curved; some single, others joining to form sprigs. To fill the gaps, draw berries, singly or in pairs, some floating free and others attached by small stalks to the leaves.*

5 *Using a medium-sized brush, paint the leaves and stems green, leaving the central midrib white. Allow to dry, then add touches of green to highlight. Allow to dry, then paint the berries red and leave to dry.*

6 *Paint the maroon background. Use a small brush to go round the leaves, stems and berries first, leaving a narrow white outline, as shown. Do not worry if the white is uneven or disappears entirely in some places. Still using the small brush, infill the awkward background spaces, then switch to a medium-sized brush for the rest. Allow to dry.*

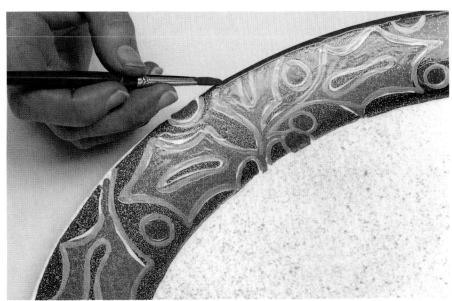

7 *Using a medium-sized brush, paint a gold outline around the leaves and berries, and along one side of the stems. Try to leave as much white outline as possible exposed, though the gold and white can overlap here and there. Leave to dry.*

Using the edge of a scalpel blade, carefully lift the central masking paper off the middle of the plate.

8 *Lightly spray the platter gold. You can spatter it by rubbing your thumb over a toothbrush dipped in gold paint, or use a miniature spray gun, available from art stores. For the gun, mix 2 parts paint to 1 part turpentine, so it is the consistency of milk. Pour the paint into the jar provided, and screw on the spray head. Use the same mixture for spattering, but only pour a little at a*

time into a shallow saucer for dipping the toothbrush in. Practise first on scrap paper, until you're happy with the effect and density of cover.

Place the platter on a large area of newspaper, and spray or spatter with gold. Leave to dry.

Paint a narrow red band around the rim, if wished. Leave to dry, then coat the paint with varnish or glaze.

HERALDIC WALL PLATE

The fleur-de-lis, Flower de Luce or heraldic lily, once symbolized the royal arms of France and, by association, France itself, but has long been a purely ornamental motif. Its unique shape is variously said to resemble an iris, the head of a sceptre, or a battle-axe! Any simple, heraldic device could be substituted, placed at regular intervals around the rim, or as a large, central feature.

The colour scheme of this decorative wall plate is inspired by the rich colours of Medieval tapestries, but you could substitute a deep, lapis-lazuli blue for the red. Water-based ceramic paints are unsuitable, as they are not available in metallic colours and should not be diluted. Solvent-based paints, however, give the results required, including the delicate colour washes.

Draw a plan before you start of your intended pattern and colour scheme. The elements of the design can be used in a variety of permutations so you could decorate each piece individually if you want.

For an integrated opulent room setting, this heraldic-inspired china was created to match the richly coloured fabrics, complete with gold detail and tassels. A variety of design options is possible: the red plate (shown in the step-by-steps) has a gold fleur-de-lis on the border with circled gold pattern on the main body area. The green version changes the colour and reverses the device pattern. Decorative bowls and coffee cups are a bright and witty addition to the range.

Tools and materials

Large shallow, white-glazed plate

Self-sticking dots

Scissors

Brushes: medium; fine

Turpentine or clear rubbing alcohol

Scalpel

Pencil: hard

Tracing paper

Compass

Carbon paper

Masking tape

Palette: red; yellow; gold; black; green

Paint used: solvent-based ceramic paint

Polyurethane varnish or glaze

1 *Stick small, sticky-backed dots (available from stationers) randomly over the middle of the plate. Cut some dots in half, and stick round the natural edge of the centre, where it meets the rim. Press them down firmly.*

2 *Paint a small area of the centre thick yellow. Dip the brush in turpentine or rubbing alcohol and spread the solvent-based ceramic paint, for a colour-washed effect. Work outward to the natural edge. Leave to dry.*

3 *Remove the dots, using the edge of a scalpel. If any yellow has bled under the dots, use a fine brush dipped in solvent to remove it.*

4 *Using the same colour-washing technique, paint the rim red. Paint up to the yellow; do not worry if you go slightly over it. Leave to dry.*

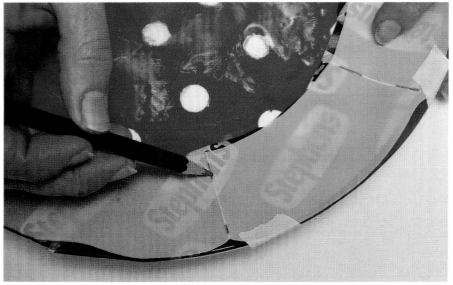

5 *Draw around the rim of the plate onto tracing paper. Measure and draw the central circle of the plate onto the paper with a compass. Cut the outer ring of tracing paper out and fold into 1/8ths; these folds mark the points of the tops of the 8 fleur-de-lis. Cut a carbon paper ring the same size, place it, face down, on the plate rim, and fix with masking tape. Open the tracing paper out and place it on the rim, fixing it with masking tape. Using a hard pencil, mark the 8 points onto the plate. Remove carbon and tracing paper.*

6 Draw a fleur-de-lis, slightly smaller than the depth of the rim, onto a small tracing paper square. Cut a square of carbon paper the same size. Position the motif, aligning the fleur-de-lis point with a mark. Hold in place with masking tape, slip the carbon paper underneath and hold it in place with your finger. Using a hard pencil, transfer the motif onto the plate. Repeat.

7 Using gold paint, paint the fleur-de-lis motifs, the centres of the white dots, and dots between the fleur-de-lis. Gold ceramic paint is quite translucent, and you may have to paint 2 coats, especially over the red, to achieve a rich tone. Allow to dry between coats.

8 Using a fine brush and black paint, outline the motifs and dots. Leave to dry.

9 Using a medium-sized brush, paint a green line around the edge of the yellow circle. Try to keep the line as even as possible. You may find it easier with a fine brush, going round 2 or 3 times. Cover the paint with varnish or glaze.

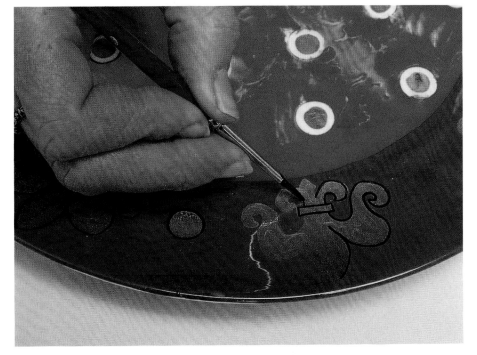

TILED WINDOW BOX

Tiled window boxes filled with elaborate, seasonal planting schemes were popular in Victorian times. This bright, sunny yellow and rich blue contemporary version is Mediterranean in feel, especially reminiscent of Portuguese exterior tile decoration. Its colours provide instant inspiration for planting: bright yellow and blue polyanthus and blue hyacinths in spring; dwarf yellow and blue iris in warm winter zones; bright blue lobelia and yellow French marigolds, nasturtiums or dwarf dahlias in summer and autumn. If you are not a keen gardener, plant yellow-variegated ivy, such as 'Goldheart', and dwarf euonymus, for year-round colour.

The window box shown is 22.5cm/9in deep, allowing a depth of 1 15 × 15cm/6 × 6in tile and 1 15 × 7.5cm/6 × 3in border tile. If you use different-sized tiles, adjust the measurements accordingly. If you make the box yourself, use hardwood and make sure you get exactly the right length screw. It is best to make the box first and then cover it with tiles. Whether you make or buy your box, decide on the number of tiles you will need. The one shown here is 5 tiles long and 1½ tiles (i.e. 1 square tile and 1 border tile) high. Allow a little extra for grout between each tile. The end panels, when finished, should be 1 square and 1 border tile wide and the same high, also allowing for the grout.

This project is drawn freehand. It is then painted using stencils and masking paint, but if you are comfortable doing so, draw the patterns directly onto the tile, then paint freehand. Since the box has to stand up to the elements, water-based ceramic paint is best, with a layer of varnish.

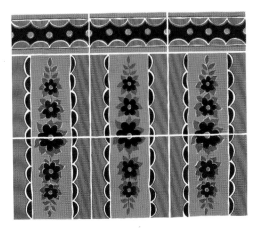

The colour scheme of this Mediterranean-style window box could also complement painted wooden shutters and doors and would look well against brick, stucco, wood or stone façades. You could substitute pastels, or neutral blacks, greys and beiges, which are less strident and less limiting in choice of plant material. And instead of the geometric motif, you could choose one based on leaf and flower shapes.

Tools and materials

8 square tiles, 15cm/6in

8 edging tiles, 15 × 7.5cm/6 × 3in

Cartridge paper

Pencils: hard; soft

Carbon paper

Metal ruler

Tracing paper

Masking tape

Masking paper

Scalpel

Cutting board

Brushes: medium; fine

Masking fluid

Palette: sunny yellow; rich dark blue

Paint used: water-based ceramic paint*

Grouting (from decorators' suppliers)

Polyurethane varnish

* requires baking

The easiest way to begin a large project like this is to sketch a design and draw it out life-size on carbon and cartridge paper. Plan it out, as shown in the illustration, as if all the sides of the box have been tiled and laid flat in a long row, with the front of the box in the middle and the 2 sides on each end.

Starting with the tile in the middle, sketch a 7.5cm/3in-wide stripe running down the centre of the tile. Repeat on the rest of the tiles, and fill in each stripe to indicate it will be blue. Put a mark below every other blue stripe, again starting with the centre tile. The marked stripes are the ones that will form a base for the diamond pattern with dots. The others will have the plain diamond design. A scroll pattern covers the adjoining tile borders.

Now draw on the full pattern starting with the centre stripe. To make it easier, draw a line down the centre of the stripe and across the middle. Use these as guidelines to keep the design geometric. Draw on a panel of both diamond patterns, and a panel of the scroll once only, so that an area the size of 2 tiles is covered. Now add the border scroll pattern. At the ends, draw an extra curve to end the pattern. The same applies to the side pieces. Using a hard pencil, trace the design (except the border) onto tracing paper and transfer the sequence onto the rest of the panels to form a repeat pattern. Alternate the diamonds and flip over the scroll tracing to mirror the image.

1 *Once you have drawn out the whole design, you can begin to trace it onto the tiles. Lay your tiles out in a row to match your drawing. Using carbon paper the same size as the tracing, transfer the design onto the tiles, working on 3 or 4 stripes at a time. Stick the carbon paper carbon-side down on the tile using masking tape. Stick the tracing paper on top and, using a hard pencil, begin the transfer.*

2 *On the stripes which are to be decorated with diamonds (the blue pattern), stick down 2 rectangles of masking paper, 8cm/3½in wide, to cover the white stripe either side.*

3 *Referring back to the plan, cut out and remove the masking paper over all those areas that are blue, using a sharp scalpel. Remember to leave the masking paper over the white vertical stripes, and rub along the edges of the remaining masking paper.*

4 *Using a medium-sized brush and masking fluid, thickly paint in the scroll shape. Leave to dry.*

5 *Paint both blue stripes. Work carefully from top to bottom and try to achieve a flat, even coat. Leave to dry.*

6 *Paint the yellow stripe, working from top to bottom and aiming for a flat, even tone. Paint carefully along the edge, to leave a straight-edged white gap.*

7 *Run a scalpel blade along the edges of the masking paper, to pierce the paint. Then, using the point of a scalpel, ease up the edges of the masking paper over both blue stripes and remove. If any paint has bled remove with a scalpel blade.*

8 *Run your scalpel carefully along both edges of the masking fluid, then, still using the scalpel, lift the dried fluid and peel it off. Scratch off any stubborn bits, if necessary. Bake both tiles.*

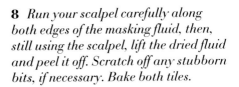

9 *Using a small brush and dark blue paint, outline the white scroll. The dark blue helps integrate the design.*

10 *Using a small brush, paint yellow centres inside the small white diamonds, and the half diamonds at the bottom and top of the tiles. Leave to dry, then bake and varnish. Repeat the process, from Step 1 on, until you have as many tiles as you need.*

Border tiles

1 *Going back to the original cartridge paper, trace the tile edge design. Cut out the tracing paper and a piece of carbon paper slightly larger than the design. Lay the carbon paper, carbon-side down on the design, tape in place, then lay the tracing paper over the top and fix with tape. Using a hard pencil, transfer the image onto the tiles. Lift off the tracing and carbon paper.*

2 *Cut strips of masking paper 16.5cm/ 6½in long and 1.5cm/½in wide. Remove the backing paper and stick down along the outer edge of the pencil line, rubbing the edge with your finger.*

Using a medium-sized brush and masking fluid, thickly paint the scrolls and dots. Leave to dry.

3 *Using blue paint and a medium-sized brush, paint the tiles, stroking in one direction, to achieve as flat and evenly dense a coat as possible. Leave to dry.*

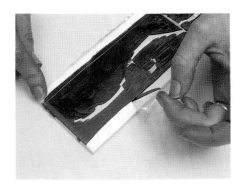

4 *Using the point of a scalpel, ease up the edges of the masking paper. Run the blade along the edges first, to pierce the paint. If any paint has bled under the masking paper, remove with a scalpel blade or small brush dipped in water.*

5 *Run your scalpel carefully along both edges of the masking fluid scrolls, then, still using the scalpel, lift the dried fluid and peel it off. Repeat with the dots. Scratch off any stubborn bits, if necessary. Bake the tiles.*

6 *Paint the edge stripes yellow, right up to the blue. Paint the dots and scrolls yellow, leaving a rough white border. Leave to dry, then bake and varnish. Repeat the process until you have all the border tiles you need.*

CERAMICS, MATERIALS AND TECHNIQUES

This book shows you how to hand-paint and decorate mass-produced, ready-glazed and -fired ceramics. The craft of the potter is as ancient as civilization, but until recently the ability to paint ceramics was limited to those designers with access to a kiln. Now, ranges of paint are available which can be 'set' in an ordinary oven, so that everyone has everything he or she needs to create decorated china in his or her own home. The results can be made durable and washable, so the items are practical as well as beautiful. The great attraction of buying ceramics to decorate yourself is that there is a huge range of ready-glazed white china available, both plain and with low-relief. This section describes all the objects, crockery, blanks and tiles that can be used; and all the materials, equipment and basic painting techniques that you need to transform the china into wonderful and personal designer creations.

Plain white china is transformed by paint – china blanks are available in a huge variety of different shapes and sizes, so you can paint everything from a huge integrated decorative service to individual pots and vases.

WORKING WITH CERAMICS

'Ceramic' is simply clay fired at a high temperature. The form a ceramic takes affects both its decoration and use, so as well as artistic considerations of shape, there are practical ones too.

The word 'ceramic' embraces a range of clay types. Earthenware is unvitrified clay (not fused, like glass, in firing), so it remains porous unless glazed. It is relatively cheap and retains heat well, and is often used for cooking dishes, such as casseroles, moulds and mixing bowls. There are many types of earthenware, including creamware, which is cream-coloured with a fine texture, and fine bone china, which is made of clay mixed with bone ash.

Porcelain is made of vitrified (completely fused, like glass) china clay, and is acid-resistant and non-porous, even when unglazed. Though heatproof, porcelain cracks if exposed to rapid temperature changes. Harder than bone china, it is expensive and is used for tableware, especially tea and dinner services, and kitchenware such as gratin dishes and fondue pots.

Stoneware is semi-vitrified and non-porous. It is fired at a higher temperature and is more expensive than earthenware, and is used for making casseroles, bowls, storage jars and tableware.

Lastly, there is terracotta, a reddish clay which is inexpensive, quite porous and usually left unglazed. In the kitchen terracotta is used for containers, pots and milk coolers, but is better known as the traditional material of flowerpots, planters and window boxes.

CERAMIC OBJECTS

Unlike tiles, three-dimensional objects have a huge diversity of shapes and uses. If the object to be decorated has a specific function, then the type of ceramic and the shape should be suitable; an umbrella stand, for example, should be stable and made of thick ceramic. Shape is also related to style, and although some shapes such as round dinner plates are classic, and can be decorated to fit into any decor, others have definite 'period' connotations: the organic, almost kidney-shaped dinner plates of the Fifties, for example, or the ornate silhouettes of Victoriana and the streamlined curves of the Thirties and Forties.

Zigzags and dots have been painted on these pots, but you could do simple triangles, undulating lines, perhaps with a leaf in each curve, or simply dots, in two colours or in varying sizes. You could decorate the rim alone, but keep in mind the type of plant – arching or trailing plants would all but hide the rim. You could simply paint the entire pot and inside rim a solid colour or, more subtly, with a watercolour-like wash to give a slight tint to the basic terracotta. (See the project on page 102 for detailed instructions.)

Most ceramic objects come under the category of 'crockery': general kitchenware for decoration, serving, eating or storing food. Remember, though, that no ceramic surface that comes in contact with food or the mouth should be painted, so unless you adapt the design to use special vitrifiable paints for firing, either use the article for decorative purposes only, perhaps hanging it on a wall or displaying it in a cabinet, or adapt the design to leave the inner surfaces and rims blank.

A good source of plain, reasonably priced white ceramic kitchenware is a restaurant supply shop, where you can often buy single items. Factory outlets and seconds or reject shops are worth trying; though you obviously

A plain white storage jar can be custom-painted to hold a variety of ingredients (see project on page 76).

have to look carefully, imperfections can often be concealed with ceramic paints, and you can buy better-quality ceramics than you might otherwise be able to do.

Kitchen shops are great places for browsing in, and specialist ceramics shops, especially Portuguese importers, often carry white-glazed ceramics and decorative objects. Although these are usually displayed or used as they are, there is no reason why you can't decorate them further to match the style of your home. Some craft shops sell china 'blanks', especially manufactured for decorating, such as ceramic jars, boxes and display plates. Chain-store, department and 'lifestyle' shops also carry inexpensive, simple ceramics, often marketed as 'setting up home' or 'starter' ranges. Don't turn your nose up at cheap hardware, D.I.Y. or discount shopping centres either: their own-brand policies and high turnover keep prices down and plain white ceramics in simple shapes needn't look cheap when painted, however low their initial cost.

The list of ceramics suitable for decorating could go on for pages, and the following is just a guideline: plates; cups and saucers; mugs; cereal, soup, serving, sugar and mixing bowls; tea and coffee pots; pitchers and jugs; serving dishes; soup tureens; cake stands; oval 'eared' fish and gratin dishes; round or oval, shallow sole dishes; round, deep baking dishes; egg cocottes; pudding basins; ramekins, including pretty heart-shaped types, and ones with handles; shallow and deep soufflés, in individual and large sizes; rectangular, round-edged lasagne dishes; salt and pepper mills; pâté pots; storage jars; oval and rectangular terrines; jelly moulds; pie dishes; lidded butter dishes; long, oval, wide-rimmed salmon dishes; sauceboats; oyster plates, with hollows for the oysters; shell-shaped scallop dishes and ice cream dishes; round cheese domes; mustard pots; snail dishes; pear-shaped avocado shells, and corn-shaped corn holders. Other ceramic objects include tiles, candlesticks, umbrella stands, vases, lamp bases, ashtrays, flowerpots, *cache pots*, soap dishes and decorative sculptures.

If you are new to painting ceramics, it is best to start on an inexpensive flat plate, then, when you feel more confident, try rounded surfaces, such as bowls, cups and teapots and, should you wish, finer-quality ceramics. Always wash and dry before painting.

CERAMIC BLANKS

Some china manufacturers cater for the craft market, and produce a wide range of plain white, glazed ceramics specifically for hand-painting. It is worth sending for a catalogue; your local craft shop can then order what you want direct. A few of the items are copies of ornate antique ceramics – though they may be attractive in their blank state, unless you are very skilled indeed, it is difficult to combine such ornate formality with the relaxed, informal approach of this book. Simple, timeless shapes tend to be best.

Blank plates come in various sizes and shapes, some with scalloped and perforated or lacy edging, in the manner of Leedsware or Bavarian open-work. Blank shallow bowls and sweet dishes are available in round, oval, rectangular, moon, heart, butterfly, leaf and basket shapes, and even three-dimensional swan, umbrella and shell shapes, again some with woven, lacy or scalloped edges. There are simple handled mugs and beer steins, cups and saucers, footed ceramic goblets and demitasse cups, for painting singly or in sets.

Blank ceramic serving accessories include pitchers, coffee pots, teapots, sugar bowls, creamers, and complete coffee and tea services. There are punch bowls with china ladles, lidded and unlidded bowls, gravy boats and jugs, butter dishes, celery dishes, hors-d'oeuvre platters, cheese boards and covers, cruets and breakfast sets of plates with 'built-in' cups. Cake plates are plain or ornately edged, and can be flat, on a pedestal or tiered, and matching ceramic cake slicers are available. Shallow-rimmed, ceramic serving trays come in various shapes and sizes, some with handles.

Glazed white ceramics, known as 'blanks' in the trade, come in a rich range of shapes, sizes and functions. Most department stores and kitchen shops have a basic selection, but some ceramics manufacturers specialize in craft supplies, and make decorative blanks such as ceramic wall plaques, Christmas tree ornaments and desk sets. If you are new to the craft, start with a flat surface, such as a plate or serving platter, or tile.

There are many styles of blank vases, but if you genuinely intend to use them for flowers, select simple shapes with relatively wide necks; narrow-necked vases give flower arrangements a pinched-in look. Blank ceramic wall plaques, for use in much the same way as blank canvas, come in round, oval, square, rectangular, diamond and shield shapes. Candleholders come in various heights and in classic and modern styles. You can buy plain white ceramic picture frames, and also trivets, for resting hot pots or pans on; both are simple projects to start with.

Tiny ceramic accessories to paint include salt and pepper sets, ceramic napkin holders and rings, toothpick holders, mustard pots, spoon rests, pill boxes, place-card holders, thimbles, pin trays and coasters, pen holders, letter openers, stamp and paper clip boxes, switch plates for walls and

White china doorplates and doorknobs can be painted. Here, masking paper covered the central panel while the turquoise rim was painted, then it was peeled off and the main design drawn on and painted. The china was sponged very lightly with cream to give an aged effect.

An American country vase with horizontal concentric bands of geometric pattern in earthy shades of tan, blue, red and white (see project on page 96).

even tooth-fairy boxes, for a child to put under his or her pillow. Small ceramics aren't necessarily easier to paint than larger ones, however, and unless you are skilled enough to do designs in miniature, tiny objects can be quite limiting to paint.

Bathroom and beauty accessories include hand mirrors set in ceramic backs, pomanders, perfume sets, ring trays, tissue box covers, toothbrush holders and soap dishes.

Many suppliers also provide blank ceramic piggy banks for children and even ceramic wall hooks shaped like teddy bears for them to hang their clothes on. Blank ceramic Christmas tree decorations include thin flat bells, stars, birds, and hearts, with holes for threading ribbons through.

CERAMIC TILES

Ceramic tiles can be used to cover areas varying from narrow, single-width, ribbon-like friezes or borders to huge walls. They are usually square or rectangular, but hexagonal and interlocking tiles are also available. Tiny, mosaic-like ceramic tiles are marketed pre-set into larger square units or fixed onto a mesh backing, for easy fixing. Machine-made tiles are cheaper and more uniform than hand-made tiles, whose unevenness and slight variations in size and colour have great character but make it more difficult to get a smooth, flush painted finish. Tiles can be glazed or unglazed and, if necessary, unglazed ceramics can be coated with a special undercoat filler to make them non-porous. Tiles can also be textured or smooth, the latter being obviously better for painting.

Ceramic tiles come in many plain colours but white, like white canvas, generally gives the best background for paints, with no colour distortion. Tiles with a small-scale corner motif or border can provide ready-made detailing for motifs to be painted or stencilled in the central area. Then, too, solid-coloured tiles can work well with applied textural effects, such as sponging; pale blue tiles could be sponged pale grey or white, for example, or rich blue tiles sponged black.

Coloured grouting is fashionable, and when done to high standards, can be exciting; though if it is less than perfect, it can look messy and stain the tiles. Coloured grouting also prevents an area of tiles being treated as one homogeneous blank canvas, when creating a large image or mural.

In the home, most ceramic tiles are permanent, built into the architecture as floor or wall surfacing. They are hard-wearing and easy to clean, so are often used behind work surfaces, for lining bath or shower areas or as splashbacks behind ovens, sinks and hand-basins. Tile fireplace surrounds also have a practical basis, in that they can be easily wiped clean of soot. Individual tiles can be painted decoratively and used to border table and counter work surfaces and, on a smaller scale, as individual heatproof teapot stands, or even as door number plates.

Tiles come in various strengths, and it is important to match a tile's strength to its location and intended use. Walls are subject to little pressure and abrasion. Bathroom and dining room floors are subject to moderate wear and tear. Kitchen and hallway floors are subject to more wear and tear, while patio, terrace and balcony paving is subject to weather as well as feet, and tiles must be heavy-duty and frostproof. Tiles for window boxes, unheated greenhouses and outdoor ornamental and swimming pools must also be frost-resistant. Interior tiles are usually manufactured specifically for floors or walls, the latter thinner and with a more delicate glaze than the former, so always state the intended use when buying tiles. Tiles for worktops, such as kitchen counters, should be acid-resistant. Good-quality satin tiles have the best painting surface.

The simple, blue and white colour scheme and leaf and tendril motif of these tiles are inspired by Portuguese ceramics. To make them, first work out how many tiles each side needs, then draw the design onto paper, at the size required. Trace the design onto the tiles as described on page 150 and paint.

D.I.Y. centres and special tile shops are the most usual source of tiles. Specialist importers of, say, Spanish, Portuguese or Italian tiles may not have plain white styles, but are worth browsing in anyway, as a source of inspiration. (Try to get a copy of their catalogue!)

Walls and floors to be tiled must be clean, dry, stable and relatively even. If the wall is uneven or deliberately curved, then small, mosaic-like tiles are best. Concrete floors are generally better than wooden floors, which tend to move, causing tiles to crack or lift. Floors of ordinary boards should first be lined with plywood or medium-density fibreboard, nailed at frequent intervals to the boards. Ceramic tiles can be set within hardwood battens, or a wooden floor could have a margin of tiles. Carpet can also be set in a tiled surround, with the tiles and carpet flush against each other.

Tiles can also be painted *in situ*, which is the easiest way to transform an area without the cost and labour involved in retiling. Decorate with solvent-based ceramic paint or acrylic paint. Coat the painted tiles with a few coats of polyurethane varnish to seal them completely. The tiles are then durable, but cleaning with abrasives should still be avoided. If you can paint tiles before mounting them – using water-based ceramic paint and baking according to the instructions on page 144 – then they are completely resistant.

mixing palette

goose feather
or feather

decorators'
paintbrush

tape measure

paint brushes

sponge

metal ruler

pencils

marker pen

WINSOR & NEWTON

A QUARELLE
Fluide
artistique de
masquage

A QUARELLFARBE
Maskiergummi,
flüssig

A CUARELA
Fluido para enmascarar pintura

WATER COLOUR
Art Masking
Fluid

75 ml ℮ 2.5 US fl.oz.

Liquitex®

ACRYLIC

ARTIST
COLOR

CADMIUM
RED LIGHT
VALUE 4.9

ROUGE DE CADMIUM CLAIR
ROJO DE CADMIO CLARO
ROSSO CADMIO CHIARO
KADMIUMROT (HELL)
#152

NET
2 FL. OZ. (59 ML.)

CAUTION:
READ BACK PANEL

BINNEY
&SMITH

solvent-based
cold ceramic
paint

scalpel

miniature spray gun

water-based
cold ceramic
paint

masking tape

acrylic paint

polyurethane varnish

MATERIALS AND EQUIPMENT

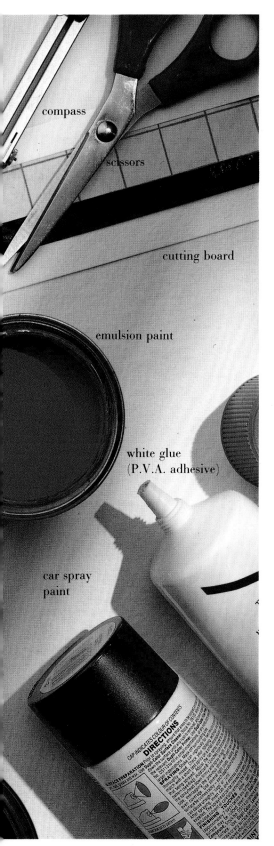

compass

scissors

cutting board

emulsion paint

white glue
(P.V.A. adhesive)

car spray
paint

You probably already have many of the materials and equipment you need for painting ceramics among your normal household supplies. Many items can be improvised, but some materials, such as paints, have to be specially purchased.

SAFETY FIRST

As well as considering the aesthetic qualities of a particular type of paint for your design, consider also the practicalities: whether, for instance, the paint can stand up to the level of wear and tear expected. Most importantly, however, you must consider safety factors. Names and applications of the various paints available vary from brand to brand, so always read the label and any information, instructions and warnings on or in the packaging.

The acrylic water-based paints and the solvent-based or cold ceramic paints described below are non-toxic. However, most laws relating to food are very stringent and these paints, as well as protective varnishes, should not be applied to surfaces that may come into direct contact with the mouth or with food. Thus, plates, the

rims of mugs, teapots and jugs, and the insides of bowls, should not be painted or glazed. This book is about purely decorative painting, and if you do want to decorate ceramics for daily use, for food or drink, then you need to adapt the designs and ideas given here for use with traditional vitrifiable pottery paints, glazes and procedures, including high-temperature kiln firing. A more detailed guide is given on page 156, and of course there are several specialized books on the subject available.

PAINTS AND VARNISH

A variety of paints can be used on glazed and fired ceramic surfaces. In this book, special water-based and solvent-based ceramic paints have been used. These are specially formulated ranges of paint designed specifically for use on mass-produced, glazed ceramics, and are perfect for the projects shown in this book. Some suppliers are given on page 158.

Solvent-based cold ceramic paints

These solvent-based paints, especially designed for use on ceramics, are called 'cold' because they are not

Hand-painting china is a craft that requires relatively little equipment, all obtainable from artists' and craft supply shops. Some specific items are required or recommended, shown left and described on the following pages, and some addresses are given on page 158.

fired. The solvent evaporates, once applied, to leave the colour in place as painted. When painted onto a non-porous surface, such as glazed white china, these paints can be wiped off, but only with a solvent. They take about 24 hours to dry after application. One readily available brand is *Ceramic à Froid*.

The painted surface will stand washing, if done very gently and very occasionally, but is not for everyday wear, as it scratches off easily. However, once dry, a decorative varnish or glaze can be added for a lustrous surface and a degree of extra protection. These glazes are often sold with the paints. Polyurethane varnish is ideal, and extremely effective for protecting *in situ* tiles. However, solvent-based cold ceramic paint is incompatible with the chemicals used in grouting, so it is unsuitable for the mosaic project on page 111, and for decorating tiles before they are grouted.

Water-based ceramic paints

These special ceramic paints are brighter than their solvent-based equivalents, come in a wide range of colours, and can be mixed for further choice of colour. They have a thermal resin acrylic that, when heated, renders the paint indelible. Though water-soluble, the paints should not be diluted more than 20 per cent with water, as the acrylic viscosity is affected, so any thinning is generally best avoided. One readily available brand is *Ceramic à l'Eau*. The paint can be applied to porous, unglazed

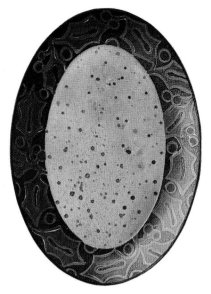

Holly and ivy, two traditional Christmas symbols, together with burnt orange berries provide the inspiration for this Christmas platter (see project on page 120).

ceramics as well as glazed, non-porous ceramic surfaces, and a better adherence can often be achieved on a rough surface.

Once the ceramic object is painted, leave it to dry thoroughly, at least overnight and up to 4 days for thickly applied paint. Place the object in a cold oven, then switch it on to 180–200°C/375–400°F/Gas Mark 5–6. Bake for at least 30 minutes, although up to 2 hours is fine, then leave the ceramic to cool in the switched-off oven. The paint, once hardened in this way, is extremely durable, and can be used in bathrooms, showers, kitchens and even on ashtrays.

Before baking your first project, it is sensible to paint an odd tile or chipped plate with the colours you are going to use to test the oven. If the paint is baked for too long or at too high a temperature it will turn brown; insufficient time or heat results in the paint not hardening and possibly

blistering or cracking if it is not air-dried properly before being baked.

If you want to build up layers of paint, such as a background colour with patterns on top, bake each layer separately. And, in the same way, colours that touch each other can be painted sequentially, and baked between applications.

Acrylic paints

A wide range of acrylic paints can be used on ceramics, though they are not specifically designed for such use. They include opaque, rich colours available in glossy, matt or pearly finish. Acrylic paints adhere well, but are for decorative use only and are best coated with at least 1 coat of polyurethane varnish, though 2 coats are needed for them to be washable. Treated with polyurethane, acrylic-painted tiles will stand up to grouting.

Car spray paints

These are perfect for stencilling tiles, but often contain toxic substances, such as lead, so are unsuitable for tableware. Car spray paints come in a wide range of colours, including metallic ones. They are extremely durable. Painted tiles, if coated with polyurethane varnish, are washable and resistant to grouting.

Quick-drying stencil paints

These are for decorative use only, and are not washable unless coated with 2 or 3 layers of polyurethane varnish. Once varnished, painted tiles will stand up to grouting but should never be soaked in water.

Enamel paints

These paints do work well on ceramic surfaces, and give a smooth, hard covering. However, they do contain lead and are unsuitable for any item of tableware. They are very durable, and a great variety of shades and colours are available.

Vitrifiable paints

These traditional ceramic paints are made of colouring agents and a base, usually containing sand or silica, minium (red lead), and borax. When fired in a high-temperature pottery kiln, the colourants develop their final colour and the borax creates the glossy finish and helps the paint to adhere to the glazed surface. Vitrifiable paints are available in powdered or liquid form and, once fired, are highly durable. Some projects in this book can be adapted to use such paints, but will then need to be fired; see page 156 for more information.

Polyurethane varnish and glazes

Varnish comes in matt or gloss finish. In this book polyurethane varnish is used with quick-drying stencil paint, acrylic paint, solvent-based ceramic paint and car spray paint. Always read the instructions before use, and use in a well-ventilated room. Apply evenly, using a large, flat brush and stroking in one direction. The more coats you apply, the more durable and washable the surface, but keep each coat thin, allowing a minimum of 4 hours' drying time between coats. Polyurethane varnish is unsuitable for ceramic surfaces that may come in contact with food or the mouth.

Manufacturers of solvent-based cold ceramic paints (such as *Ceramic à Froid*) also supply a gloss-only glaze specifically designed for use with the paint, to make it more durable and resistant.

TOOLS AND EQUIPMENT
Paintbrushes

A wide range of sizes and shapes are available, from fine, pointed brushes for delicate or detailed work, to broad, flat brushes for covering large areas with tone. Real sable brushes are lovely to work with, but they are a luxury and, for most work, unnecessary. Soft, imitation sable brushes are fine. Avoid hard brushes as they will leave bristle marks, which can be especially annoying on flat areas of colour. You can buy special round stencil brushes in a variety of sizes, with stiff, short bristles cut square; these give a stippled effect.

Decorators' brushes come in larger sizes than artists' brushes, and are ideal for painting large flat areas or large-scale designs. Toothbrushes can also be used as a stencil brush to stipple paint onto a surface.

Feathers can also be used, particularly for marbling effects. The end of the feather is dipped into paint and then gently dragged over the painted

Car spray paint is quick to apply and dry, long-lasting, and excellent for covering large surfaces. A range of subtly different effects can be achieved, depending on the distance and angle from the object being sprayed.

surface to give the effect of veining.

Always clean brushes immediately after use, either in soapy water or solvent, according to the type of paint, and re-form pointed brushes into a sharp point to dry. To keep round stencil brushes in perfect shape while drying, wrap a rubber band around them. Never leave brushes to soak in liquid as it will destroy their shape. Dry them upright in a jar, so there is no pressure on the bristles. Before using, gently flick the bristles with your thumb to dislodge loose bristles or bits of dust.

Spray guns

A miniature spray gun can be purchased from arts and crafts stores. Different densities of paint can be achieved by pressing the button hard or softly – and by spraying close to the object or at a distance.

The spray gun shown on page 142 is an even smaller version, which works by filling the vessel with paint and blowing through the tube to spray paint out the other end.

Palette

A plate or saucer will do for holding small quantities of paint or for mixing on, but inexpensive, plastic rectangular trays, subdivided by shallow rims into sections, are more useful for keeping paints separate, as well as providing several receptacles for mixing small quantities of paint. A white or pale, neutral-coloured palette lets you see the individual colours clearly; strongly coloured palettes can cause colour distortion.

Scalpel

Also called a craft or an X-acto knife, this is a lightweight, small knife that is held like a pen and can be controlled very accurately for detailed work. The disposable blades come in many shapes and are replaced when blunt. Short, triangular, sharply pointed blades are best.

Cutting surface

For cutting out stencils, you need a hard, level cutting surface. Best are the purpose-made cutting boards or mats that are available from art and graphic design shops. Alternatively, you can use a scrap piece of formica or melamine. Wood is less suitable as it quickly blunts scalpel blades and makes it difficult to cut out a design accurately.

Marker pen

Fine-nibbed, graphic designers' pens are useful for marking out points around the rim of an object to be painted. These points serve as guides to spacing patterns, especially repeat ones. Marker pens are sold in art supply stores and some stationers. Water-soluble, black ink is best; waterproof inks can usually be removed with a dab of turpentine applied with a clean rag or tissue.

Pencils

For marking directly onto ceramic surfaces, soft pencils such as a 2B, 4B and 6B are best, but for carbon-paper transfers, an H or 2H is preferable.

Masking fluid

Watercolour art masking fluid contains ammonia and rubber latex, and it is used to mask out areas that need protecting while you paint another area. Always shake the bottle thoroughly before using, and use a paintbrush to apply to a clean, dry surface. Masking fluid is toxic, so wash the brush and your hands thoroughly after each use, and store well out of reach of children. It is easily lifted off after use.

Carbon paper

Carbon paper is used to transfer designs onto the object to be painted. It is placed, carbon-side down, onto the object, with the image drawn on tracing paper stuck over the top. With a hard pencil, draw over the image, so that the pressure transfers the image onto the ceramic surface. Most carbon paper is blue or black, which is ideal for white or pale glazes, but you can buy white carbon paper, which shows up more effectively on dark glazes.

Masking paper

This is a transparent film of self-adhesive paper that has a waxed-paper backing which peels away before use. It is available from stationers, art shops and office supply shops. Masking paper can be cut to shape to mask out areas you want to keep blank while painting. There are proprietary brands sold for artistic use, such as 'Frisk' and 'Transpaseal', but less expensive and just as effective are those sold for protecting book covers from damage.

Tracing paper

Tracing paper is used with carbon paper for transferring original designs onto the object to be painted. Artists' tracing paper, sold in art supply and specialist shops, is best.

Stencil paper

This is manila paper or card waterproofed with linseed oil. It comes in a wide range of thicknesses or gauges. The finer the gauge, the easier it is to cut, but thicker gauges are useful for patterns repeated over and over again. Stencil paper is sold in art shops. If unavailable, you could also use the rather more expensive acetate, which, being transparent, is easier to position accurately than stencil paper, though it is liable to curl with repeated use. Thick cartridge or watercolour paper can also be used for stencils, but be prepared to cut several identical stencils, since these types of paper become soggy with repeated use.

Paper tissue

This is used both for mopping up paint that has seeped onto masked-out areas, and also as a method of applying paint to get a crumpled, textural effect. Soft toilet tissue is better than kitchen paper roll for this, since the latter is too coarse.

Sponge

Sponges, with their efficient absorbency and uneven texture, allow you to achieve a wide range of interesting paint effects, depending on the amount of paint absorbed and

released, the pressure when applied and density of application. Natural sponges are better but more expensive; they have more variation in texture, are easier to scrunch up, and hold the paint better than synthetic sponges. If you do use synthetic sponges, tear them into small, irregular shapes first.

Turpentine or rubbing alcohol

Turpentine, rubbing alcohol and methylated or white (mineral) spirit are all solvents used in ceramics — primarily for cleaning brushes or for removing paint mistakes or over-runs, but also as a paint thinner to create a translucent, 'colour-washed' effect.

Masking tape

This is a self-adhesive tape, sold in rolls and in various widths. (It has several uses in graphic and interior

Masking paper is clear and self-adhesive, so is very good for cutting out and securing onto the china as a 'fixed' template to paint over. When the paint is dry, the paper is peeled off to reveal a perfect white design, which can be painted further as required.

decorating work.) In ceramic painting, it is used to achieve a hard, crisp edge, or to mask out or protect areas from paint, and also to hold stencils and tracings in place.

Airtight storage containers

It is hard to judge exactly how much paint to mix. Left-over paint exposed to air hardens, usually within 24 hours, and becomes unusable. If a project is only partly completed, mixing the identical colour again can be very difficult, if not impossible. Even if the project is complete, it is sensible to store any excess paint for future use rather than let it go to waste.

BASIC TECHNIQUES

Experiment first, if you are new to a particular technique, before attempting to decorate the ceramic object. An old plate, tile or even an old laminated shelf or cupboard door will suffice. If you feel you need plenty of practice, as you might with freehand painting, start with a sketchpad and watercolours, and work in loose, swift, relaxed strokes, until you feel confident; slow, tentative brush-strokes will look contrived and detract from the finished effect.

The difference between success and dissatisfaction can be as small a thing as a slight change of pressure or timing, or simply removing excess paint from the brush with a few strokes first. When sponging, for example, creating a professional-looking surface is often a matter of dabbing just the right amount of excess paint off the sponge before building up an easy rhythm as you cover the ceramic surface itself.

CREATING A DESIGN

Before starting to paint your china, it is best to draw out a plan of the design first on paper. All the projects in this book show a colour illustration of the planned design – and, often, alternative designs as well. If you plan to copy these designs exactly, you can use these illustrations as guidelines (see 'Transferring a design', on the next page). If you want to adapt the designs, however, or create one of your own, you will need to draw up your own plan.

Measure the ceramic object in all directions, then draw the outline onto a piece of paper or thin card, as accurately as possible and to actual size. If you are planning to paint a circumference border or rim, for example on a vase, then measure it and draw it out flat as a long rectangle. You will need to draw different views of the object if they are part of the design – if, for instance, you are painting a rim to a pot, draw an overhead circle view of the top.

Next, slowly draw in the pattern or design that you have in mind. Be careful to keep various elements of the design in balance, and distances and sizes in proportion. This plan will also be a useful colour guide when painting, so fill the different areas in with coloured crayon or annotate it.

RESIZING A DESIGN

Sometimes a design is the right size, but more often you will need to enlarge or reduce it. Using a photocopying

These tiles and decorative tea service are all painted using relatively simple techniques. Once you have mastered the general principles outlined in the following pages, designing and painting your own projects will be quite straightforward.

machine with that facility is easiest, although enlargements of more than 156 per cent may involve two stages, making a second enlargement of the first copy.

You can also draw a squared grid over the original design, then, on a second sheet of paper, make a larger or smaller grid, with the same number of squares. (If the design comes from a book, trace it onto a sheet of tracing paper first, then draw a grid over it.) Mark onto the new grid the points where the original design bisects the original grid lines, square by square, then connect up the lines. If any of the lines look awkward or disjointed, don't be afraid to improvise a little, smoothing out the curves.

To double the size of a design, overlay a 2.5cm/1in-square grid on the original, then re-draw it on a 5cm/2in-square grid. To halve the size, re-draw it on a 1.25cm/½in-square grid. You can also change the proportions of the design, by increasing or decreasing the horizontal or vertical lines unequally. This is useful if you want to use a basically square design on a long, narrow object, such as a cylindrical vase.

TRANSFERRING A DESIGN

Once you have your planned design on paper, you will need to transfer it to your ceramic object. Cut a square or rectangle of tracing paper and a similar sized one of carbon paper to give a margin of at least 2.5cm/1in around the design. Trace your design onto the tracing paper. Place the carbon paper, carbon-side down, onto the ceramic surface area to be decorated. Position the tracing paper on top, and stick both in place with small pieces of masking tape, to prevent accidental movement while the design is transferred.

Using a sharp pencil, draw over the tracing, pressing firmly and evenly to ensure that the carbon adheres to the ceramic surface. If you are repeating the pattern, slightly move the carbon paper each time so an unused area is beneath the tracing.

MASKING OUT

The following techniques are used to protect surface areas while you apply paint to adjacent ones.

Masking fluid

Watercolourists use artists' masking fluid to keep specific areas crisp and white, while allowing them to paint adjacent areas freely. This is tricky to achieve freehand, particularly for quite tiny and intricate, white areas, such as the crest of a wave or seagulls against a sky. Masking liquid can also be used on ceramics, applied quite thickly with a brush. Its semi-matt texture when dry makes it easy to see. Once dry – and this will vary depending on how thickly you apply it, but usually only a minute or two – you can paint the adjacent areas. Any paint brushed over the masking fluid will not adhere. Wait until the paint is thoroughly dry before removing the fluid by lifting one edge of the dried fluid with a scalpel and carefully pulling the stretchy substance off the ceramic, easing it away at the edges.

Artworks and templates for designs are given in the projects, but whether you use these or your own drawings, you will need to enlarge them to fit your ceramic, using a photocopier or grid method as here (described above).

Once you have your design drawn up to the size required, you will need to transfer an outline, using tracing and carbon paper, onto the china object as a painting guide.

If necessary, use the scalpel to clean up the edge line of the paint.

Masking tape

This is used to produce a hard, straight, painted edge, such as a border on a tile or around the rim of a mug. To use masking tape, first measure and mark out the width of the stripe or depth of the border at regular intervals. Lay the tape up to your markers, then press it down firmly and run your fingernail sharply along the edges of the tape to help prevent paint oozing under it.

Masking tape is helpful but not foolproof. It is safer to run brushstrokes parallel to the edge of the tape, rather than at right angles to it. As soon as the paint dries to a sticky consistency, remove the tape. Leaving the tape on until the paint is fully dry may result in the tape lifting off paint that was intentionally applied as well.

Masking paper

Waxy masking paper is difficult to draw on, but you can mark a template (the mirror image of the shape) to be cut out on the backing paper, or draw the shape onto tracing paper and then tape it on top of the masking paper and cut through both with a scalpel. Masking paper cuts easily, so proceed with caution. For cutting straight lines, cut against a metal ruler (plastic and wooden rulers will be damaged by a scalpel, ruining both the blade and the edge). If possible, protect the masking paper to be used with the ruler, so that if the blade slips, it will cut into the waste paper.

Once the shapes or edges are cut out, roughly position the masking paper on the object; then, starting at one end, peel away the backing paper and carefully stick it in place. Using your fingers or a soft cloth, press from the centre to the edges to work out

any air bubbles, then run your fingernail along every edge to fix it firmly in place. Paint your design and, as soon as the paint dries to a sticky consistency, gently insert a scalpel blade under one corner of the masking paper and ease it up and off, and discard. Any accidental seepage can be cleaned with a fine brush or bit of paper tissue dipped in water or the appropriate solvent.

STENCILLING

A stencil is a thin sheet with a decorative pattern cut out, through which paint is applied, to repeat the pattern on a chosen surface. You can buy ready-made stencils from arts and crafts shops and from mail order catalogues, and they will be either already cut out or marked for you to cut out. However, you have wider scope for creativity if you design and make your own.

A stencil, whether of firm card or, as here, of self-adhesive clear masking paper, allows you to paint or sponge on an intricate design with accuracy, leaving neat borders or outlines.

Making a stencil

For the crispest edges and longest-lasting stencils, use stencil paper or acetate (watercolour paper is adequate for only limited use). Cut the acetate or paper into a square or rectangle slightly larger than the image to be cut out; leave at least 5cm/2in between the image and the edge of the paper or acetate to maintain strength and prevent accidental tears. Using carbon paper and tracing paper (see 'Transferring a design', page 150, for technique), transfer the motif to the centre of the acetate or paper and place on a hard, flat cutting surface. Holding the paper or acetate steady, begin cutting in one corner of the motif with a scalpel, drawing the blade toward you and with your other hand behind the blade, never in front. Rotate the paper or acetate, as necessary, and try to keep the cutting motion continuous and fluid. A lot of stops and starts can leave tiny nicks in the outline.

If there is more than one colour to your motif, you can cut each colour on a separate stencil, or cut them all on the same sheet. If you cut them on separate sheets, you have to be careful positioning them. This can be done by making pin holes in the four corners and aligning them, or, on clear stencils, you can draw in corner marks. If you use a single sheet, unless 'bridges' are cut to divide each colour area, you will have to mask out some areas while you work on others.

If the motif is very complex or extensive, you may wish to break it down into simpler components, separating out the different colours onto several stencil sheets.

Tape the finished stencil securely in place, then apply paint according to the chosen technique.

PAINT TECHNIQUES AND EFFECTS

As well as freehand paint designs and fill-in pattern painting, there are a number of basic paint techniques that can be used for an all-over effect — such as a simply sponged vase — or as the background to a more elaborate design. You can, in fact, adapt most special interior design paint effects to ceramics of all kinds.

FREEHAND PAINTING

This is the easiest technique, once you have built up confidence, but it is also the most challenging, particularly when you first start. When selecting brushes, always match the size and shape of the brush to the surface area to be covered, whether by washes or fine linework. If in any doubt, choose the smaller brush.

Loading a brush with too much paint is a common beginner's mistake. Draw the full brush against the edge of a palette or across a piece of paper, to achieve the right control.

Unless you want a scumbled effect (an uneven or rough surface finish), keep your brush moving in one direction, whether from the top of the object down, or across, from one side to the other.

SPRAYING

Aerosol car spray paints and spray guns produce a covering that ranges in density from solid colour to light, misty tints, depending on the distance from the object that the spray can is held, the duration of the burst and the number of times the spray is applied. The texture is finer and more even than sponging, densest toward the middle of the area sprayed, and diffuse and misty round the edges. For high-density coverage, several light sprays are better than one heavy one.

Drips and runs are the main problem of spray painting, and can usually be avoided by spraying an expendible surface first for a few seconds to gauge the pressure, then, in a single motion, spraying the ceramic object. You may have to repeat the spray to achieve the right coverage, but always allow 30 minutes or so between each burst to prevent a drip developing. Spray paint covers a very broad area, so work on newspaper spread out well beyond the object being sprayed. Good ventilation is essential.

Sponging

Sponging is a quick, relaxed and easy technique producing an airy, highly textural effect. It is a very popular wall finish, but is equally effective on ceramics. It involves applying one or more colours onto a solid base colour, using a sponge. Applying 2 coats of a closely related, harmonious or contrasting colour is very effective and creates a good sense of depth. One coat can look uneven and patchy, unless the paint and base colour are very closely related – salmon pink and apricot, for instance. You can control the density of the paint according to the amount absorbed by the sponge and the size of the sponge holes. An open sponge produces a large-scale, rough texture, while a fine sponge produces a denser coat. The size of the sponge also affects the density, as does the amount of space that you leave between the individual sponge marks. Tissue paper screwed up into a loose ball and dipped into paint gives a similar effect.

Oversponging is a common mistake, but this can be avoided by testing out your technique on an old plate or piece of laminate.

Stippling and dragging

These, like sponging, create an interesting visual surface for an object, and are particularly effective in stencilling. They can be done in a single colour or a subtle combination for stronger impact. To stipple, hold a short, fat brush (a stencil brush is ideal) upright or at right angles to the surface and make quick dabbing motions. To drag, simply pull the brush over the surface in one direction only to create a streaked effect.

Sponging can be done with a variety of materials for different paint effects. Even screwed-up tissue will work. Always test first on a bit of scrap paper or old tile.

Verdigris

Verdigris is the green deposit on copper or brass that has been oxidized and exposed to the elements, creating a crumbled surface texture of gold, bronze, blue, green and ochre. You can try to recreate this texture with paint on ceramics; the candlesticks shown below were painted with this effect. It would also look good on vases or lamp bases. Use solvent-based cold ceramic or acrylic paints, as the paint will need to be thinned with turpentine. Here gold acrylic paint is used and then solvent-based ceramic paint for the dark and light green. Coat the finished items with varnish if liked for extra protection.

1 *Paint the object with a base colour of rich gold. Apply acrylic paint with multi-directional brushstrokes, leaving thick areas of paint for added texture. Allow to dry.*

2 *Begin building up a texture. Dip a large brush into dark green paint and, dipping the brush into turpentine or clear rubbing alcohol to thin it unevenly, daub over the object. Leave some areas of paint thin enough for the gold to show through. Leave to dry for about 10 minutes and then daub some light green paint over, so that the two colours bleed together. Leave to dry.*

3 *Lastly, wash over the verdigris to thin it out with a little turpentine to reveal the various layers of colour. Blend some dark gold or bronze paint in with this wash. Leave to dry.*

Marbling

This traditional paint effect works very well applied to ceramics; you can transform ordinary objects into quite distinguished, elegant ones. An object could be totally marbled or perhaps, as with a vase, just have a band around the neck. Marbled tiles are simple but impressive. Use solvent-based ceramic paints, or water-based and bake them for durability and washability.

1 *First of all, paint or sponge on the base colour of the marble – perhaps a rich red or green. Leave to dry if using solvent-based paint, or if using water-based, bake as described on page 144.*

2 & 3 *Put some paint into a shallow dish. Dip your sponge into water and wring it out. Dip into the paint, remove the excess by dabbing the sponge onto kitchen paper or newspaper, then sponge over the ceramic surface. Leave to dry when complete, or bake.*

4 *Apply veins, using a feather. Dip the end of the feather into white or cream paint, then lightly move it across the surface. Try not to overdo it – a few lines will be more effective. Leave to dry, or bake again.*

A NOTE ON KILN-FIRING

This book has been designed to open up the exciting craft of ceramic painting to the general home hobbyist and artist. The projects shown are created with a range of special paints and glazes that are specifically designed so that it is possible to 'fire' or heat-fix them in a domestic oven. The advantages of this are that everything you need for painting china is accessible and easily to hand in a home environment. The only disadvantage is that – as has been pointed out within the book – the items thus painted are slightly less resistant to wear than kiln-fired objects, and although the paints are officially non-toxic, the decorated item is not completely food-safe. The only way to ensure that a ceramic object is entirely food-safe is to design it so that the area to come into contact with the mouth, food or drink is left unpainted and unglazed, or to fire it at a higher temperature than is possible in a domestic oven, in other words in a kiln.

There are, essentially, two methods of firing painted ceramics. One is hard-firing, which is at the very high temperature of between 750°–1100°C for earthenware and about 1400°C for porcelain. This is for unglazed items, and fuses the paint into the base material; the result is permanent. Soft-firing (or muffled firing) is used where the paint has been applied to glazed china, and is thus more applicable to the type of designs and projects in this book. The design is painted on with special vitrifiable paints, which are traditional ceramic paints made up of colouring agents and a base, usually containing sand or silica, minium (red lead), and borax. When fired in a pottery kiln (at a temperature of 730°C for earthenware and 830°C for porcelain), the colourants develop their final colour; the borax creates a glossy finish and helps the paint to adhere to the glazed surface. Vitrifiable paints are available in powdered or liquid form,

and can be augmented by special varnishes ('lustres') and even precious metals such as gold. Once fixed, they are extremely durable. If you do plan to kiln-fire your painted objects, it is a good idea to paint and fire a sample piece first – perhaps an old tile – to test the final colour, before completing your project.

It is quite easy to find a kiln at a local craft group or pottery centre, or perhaps a local education institute, where you might be able to use the facilities for a small fee. Ask for help and advice about materials and preparation from the teacher or person in charge of kiln-firing, as kilns and conditions vary, and there may be special requirements to consider.

Another option is to consider purchasing your own kiln. This is not such an outrageous investment as it might first appear; a small studio kiln can be purchased for about £450 (UK) or $800 (USA). This is a basic model of about 1.4 cubic feet, but is in fact the largest kiln that can be run off a domestic electricity supply. Its size would restrict you to firing only one item at a time, and would disallow particularly large pieces. A larger kiln of 2.6 cubic feet, which would entail a special adaptation to the electricity supply, could cost about £600/$1100. Such a purchase is probably only worth making if you intend to paint a large number of ceramic objects for functional as well as decorative purposes.

CARE OF DECORATED CERAMICS

The paints specified in the projects in this book are generally decorative not functional, and the ceramics decorated with them are basically for display, so they should not need to be washed often or risk damage through wear and tear. That having been said, water-based ceramic paints can be oven-baked for durability and are scratch-resistant and harder-wearing than solvent-based ceramic paints. You will find that with care your painted ceramics will remain perfect for years.

For ceramic objects on display,

dusting with a soft cloth should suffice, but if washing is necessary, quickly hand wash – never use a dishwasher – in lukewarm water and a mild detergent. Avoid soaking in soapy water, which can lift the paint.

Protective, clear glazes are available for solvent-based paints, and are applied once the paint is thoroughly dry. These make painted ceramics waterproof and add a high level of durability. They are gloss, however, and some people find that this additional, reflective layer detracts from the quality of the paintwork.

A specially painted Christmas platter (see the project on page 120) forms the centrepiece of a beautiful festive display, and if treated with care, can be used year after year.

Polyurethane varnish is available in matt and gloss. Non-glazed decorated ceramic tiles, such as quarry tiles, are harder-wearing and easier to keep clean if sealed.

Glazed ceramic wall tiles should be cleaned with mild detergent or soap and water, never with acid-based or abrasive cleaning products.

SUPPLIERS AND STOCKISTS

All the paints, materials and equipment in this book are commonly available in high street art and craft shops, or from the following major manufacturers, distributors and shops:

UNITED KINGDOM

Potterycrafts Ltd, Harrison Bell, Campbell Road, Stoke-on-Trent, England ST4 4ET.
0782 272444
Potterycrafts Ltd can supply a range of white china 'blanks' and ceramic kilns, as well as the more basic materials discussed. They also organize an extensive network of ceramic painting groups and classes.

Pebeo cold ceramic paints distributed in the UK by **Art Graphique**, Unit 2 Poulton Close, Dover, Kent CT17 0HL. 304 242244

AUSTRALIA

Artery
31 Davey St
Hobart TAS 7000
002 232130

Art Smart
50 Ethel St
Seaforth NSW 2092
02 9497477

The Balcony Fine Arts and Gifts
86 Wodonga VIC 3690
060 561365

Craftree Cottage
Shop 29 Oakleigh Central
Oakleigh Vic 3166
03 5683606

E&F Good
31 Landsdowne Terrace
Walkerville SA 5081
08 3444306

Emtex Handcrafts Pty Ltd
7 Bellows Ave
Welshpool WA 6106
09 4511936

Francheville (Aust) Pty Ltd
1–5 Perry St
Collingwood VIC 3066
03 4160611

Janets Art Supplies
145 Victoria Ave
Chatwood NSW 2067
02 4178572

Oxford Art Supplies
221–223 Oxford St
Darlinghurst NSW 2010
02 3604601

Peter Sudich Custom Framing
155 Katoomba St
Katoomba NSW 2780
047 822866

Salamanca Place Gallery
67 Salamanca Place
Hobart Tas 7000
002 2333208

Speedy Art Supplies
P.O. Box 151
Sunnybank Qld 4109
07 208 0866

All Spotlight stores stock *Pebeo* products in their habadashery departments. There are 30 stores around Australia.

NORTH AMERICA

A.R.T. Studio Clay Company
1555 Louis Avenue
Elk Grove Village, IL 60007
708-593-6060
Paints

Bailey Pottery Equipment Corp.
CPO Box 1577
Kingston, NY 12401
914-339-3721
toll-free 800-431-6067
fax 914-339-5530
Paints

Ceramic Supply of New York and New Jersey, Inc.
534 LaGuardia Place
New York, NY 10012
212-475-7236
10 Dell Glen Avenue
Lodi, NJ 07644
201-340-3005
fax 201-340-0089
Paints and supplies

Contemporary Kiln Inc.
26 "O" Commercial Blvd.
Novato, CA 94949
415-883-8921
fax 415-883-2435

Duncan Ceramics
5673 East Shields
Fresno, CA 93727
209-291-2515
Paints

Laguna Clay Co.
14400 Lomitas Avenue
City of Industry, CA 91746
818-330-0631
fax 818-330-7694
Paints and supplies

Maryland China Co.
54 Main Street
Reistertown, MD 21136
301-833-5559
toll-free 800-638-3880
White china

Mid-South Ceramic Supply
1230 4th Avenue N.
Nashville, TN 37208
615-242-0300
Watercolor paints

Nationart Inc.
220 Ballardvale Street
Wilmington, MA 01877
508-657-5995
fax 508-658-2846
Pebeo paints

Trucker's Pottery Supplies Inc.
15 West Pearce Street #7
Richmond Hill, Ontario
Canada L4B 1H6
416-889-7705
fax 416-889-7707

Index

ACKNOWLEDGEMENTS

The publishers would like to thank the following for their contribution of props for photography: Markov and Beedles, Antiquarius A13 & F1, 135 Kings Road, London SW3, tel. 071 352 4545; Putnams, 55 Regents Park Road, London NW1; David Mellor, 4 Sloane Square, London SW1; Fired Earth, Twyford Mill, Oxford Road, Adderbury, Oxon OX17 3HP; Stitches & Daughters, Tranquilvale, Blackheath, London SE3; Gallery of Antique Costume & Textiles, Church Street, London NW8. In addition they would like to thank Alex Corrin for indexing.